OF LEAF AND FLOWER

{ HOLLYHOCK 'NIGRA' }

STORIES AND POEMS FOR GARDENERS

OF
LEAF
AND
FLOWER

Edited by Charles Dean and Clyde Wachsberger

Illustrations by Clyde Wachsberger

A Karen and Michael Braziller Book

PERSEA BOOKS / NEW YORK

Persea Books, Inc.
171 Madison Avenue
New York, New York 10016

Library of Congress Cataloging-in-Publication Data

Of leaf and flower : stories and poems for gardeners / edited by Charles Dean and Clyde Wachsberger ; illustrations by Clyde Wachsberger.—1st ed.
     p. cm.
  "A Karen and Michael Braziller book."
  ISBN 0-89255-269-7 (cloth : alk. paper)
    1. Gardening—Literary collections, 2. Gardeners—Literary collections. 3. Garden—Literary collections. 4. American literature. 5. English literature. I. Dean, Charles. II. Wachsberger, Clyde.

PS509.G37 O38 2001
810.8'0364—dc21   2001034645

Text set in Georgia and designed by Rita Lascaro

Manufactured in the United States of America

FIRST EDITION

CONTENTS

LIST OF ILLUSTRATIONS

Preface

We garden. Our garden on Long Island's historic North Fork surrounds our small eighteenth-century house. It is not one of those lovely gardens that, having achieved perfection some time in the past, is pristinely maintained from year to year. We're always moving things around. We like to experiment with unfamiliar plants; we like to grow from seed; we like to push hardiness limits. Most of all, we love continually to create new settings, preferably wild and complex. Our garden looked like a jungle even before we started growing bananas, plumbagos, cannas, tibouchinas, and other tropical plants. Although it is less than one third of an acre, it is a garden that demands all the time, money, and space we have. The two of us are usually out there in the thick of it.

Yet getting our chores done is complicated by endless visitors: friends, neighbors, gardeners, strangers. The first time, they might have been curious about some unusual plants visible from the street. They come back again to see the garden in different seasons or even to see it at different times of the same day. They find us muddy, sweaty, and scratched, sometimes dotted with burdock seeds or veiled against mosquitoes. Of course these guests have questions, such as: What on earth are you two otherwise apparently sane people doing?

The answers to many gardening questions can be found in how-to manuals and even in plant catalogues. But how to explain the profound passions and wild obsessions that motivate gardeners? What is it that lures us back to our gardens for one more look before dark?

We decided to turn to poets and storytellers for answers. We began by looking for themes that explore what it means to be a gardener in one's own garden. We quickly discovered masterful writers who convey the effects that a love of plants might have on any of us.

We found ourselves thinking in garden terms while we made this collection. Gardeners love new cultivars of perennial favorites, and we were delighted to find that some beloved writers had selections new to us. We've included a few heirlooms, popular generations ago but seldom seen today. Then there's always that wish for something new, so we've selected many recent works whose beauty we hope will astonish you as it has us.

We chose our title from Kathleen Raine's poem "Winifred's Garden," which describes a garden that has gone untended. Gardeners will immediately understand the complex mix of liberation and sadness expressed here, but the poem opens the experience to everyone. We believe all the works included in this collection evoke equally essential feelings that, while resonating especially with gardeners, are feelings to which any reader will respond. Here you may read about scheduling one's life by a garden's seasons, worrying over an ailing houseplant, ordering an instant garden, coveting and stealing plants, and creating uniquely potent compost.

From among the wonderful poems and stories we considered, we chose these twenty-four favorites. Our experience as gardeners helped: we've sometimes wanted to tuck in more plants than space allows but had to learn to select those that iwe can't do without. From among the many wonderful poems and stories we considered, we chose these favorites.

The *sumi* ink illustrations are portraits of plants in our garden that we especially love.

We intend to keep a stack of this book on our garden bench. We have often sent our visitors home with a cutting or a division. Now, when they ask questions too perplexing for us, we'll send them home with a book, too.

—Charles Dean and Clyde Wachsberger

OF LEAF AND FLOWER

ROBERT FROST

Leaves Compared with Flowers

A tree's leaves may be ever so good,
So may its bark, so may its wood;
But unless you put the right thing to its root
It never will show much flower or fruit.

But I may be one who does not care
Ever to have tree bloom or bear.
Leaves for smooth and bark for rough,
Leaves and bark may be tree enough.

Some giant trees have bloom so small
They might as well have none at all.
Late in life I have come on fern.
Now lichens are due to have their turn.

I bade men tell me which in brief,
Which is fairer, flower or leaf.
They did not have the wit to say,
Leaves by night and flowers by day.

Leaves and bark, leaves and bark,
To lean against and hear in the dark.
Petals I may have once pursued.
Leaves are all my darker mood.

SAKI

The Occasional Garden

"Don't talk to me about town gardens," said Elinor Rapsley; "which means, of course, that I want you to listen to me for an hour or so while I talk about nothing else. 'What a nice-sized garden you've got,' people said to us when we first moved here. What I suppose they meant to say was what a nice-sized site for a garden we'd got. As a matter of fact, the size is all against it; it's too large to be ignored altogether and treated as a yard, and it's too small to keep giraffes in. You see, if we could keep giraffes or reindeer or some other species of browsing animal there we could explain the general absence of vegetation by a reference to the fauna of the garden: 'You can't have wapiti *and* Darwin tulips, you know, so we didn't put down any bulbs last year.' As it is, we haven't got the wapiti, and the Darwin tulips haven't survived the fact that most of the cats of the neighborhood hold a parliament in the center of the tulip bed; that rather forlorn-looking strip that we intended to be a border of alternating geranium and spiraea has been utilized by the cat-parliament as a division lobby. Snap divisions seem to have been rather frequent of late, far more frequent than the geranium blooms are likely to be. I shouldn't object so much to ordinary cats, but I do complain of having a congress of vegetarian cats in my garden; they must be vegetarians, my dear, because, whatever ravages they may commit among the sweet-pea seedlings, they never seem to touch the sparrows; there are always just as many adult sparrows in the garden on Saturday as there were on Monday, not to mention newly fledged additions. There seems to have been an irreconcilable difference of opinion between sparrows and Providence since the beginning of time as the whether a crocus looks best standing upright with its roots in the earth or in a recumbent posture with its stem neatly severed; the sparrows always have the last word in the matter, at least in our garden they do. I fancy that Providence must have originally intended to bring in an amending Act, or whatever it's called, providing either for a less destructive sparrow or a more indestructible crocus. The one consoling point about our garden is that it's not visible from the drawing room or the smoking room, so unless people are dining or lunching with us they can't spy out the nakedness of the land. That is why I am so furious with Gwenda Pottingdon, who has practically forced herself on me for lunch on Wednesday next; she heard me offer the Paulcote girl lunch if she was up shopping on that day, and, of course, she asked if she might come too. She is only coming to gloat over my bedraggled and flowerless borders and to sing the praises of her own detestably over cultivated garden. I'm sick of being told it's the envy of the neighborhood; it's like everything else that belongs to her—her car, her dinner parties, even her headaches, they are all superlative; no one else ever had anything like them. When her eldest child was confirmed it was such a sensational event, according to her account of it, that one almost expected questions to be asked about it in the House of Commons, and now she's coming on purpose to stare at my few miserable pansies and the gaps in my sweet pea border, and to give me a glowing, full-length description of the rare and sumptuous blooms in her rose garden."

"My dear Elinor," said the Baroness, "you would save yourself all this heartburning and a lot of gardener's bills, not to mention sparrow anxieties, simply by paying an annual subscription to the O.O.S.A."

"Never heard of it," said Elinor; "what is it?"

"The Occasional-Oasis Supply Association," said the Baroness; "it exists to meet cases exactly like yours, cases of backyards that are of no practical use for gardening purposes, but are required to blossom into decorative scenic backgrounds at stated intervals, when a luncheon or dinner party is contemplated. Supposing, for instance, you have people coming to lunch at one-thirty; you just ring up the Association at about ten o'clock the same morning, and say, 'Lunch garden.' That is all the trouble you have to take. By twelve forty-five your yard is carpeted with a strip of velvety turf, with a hedge of lilac or red may, or whatever happens to be in season, as a background, one or two cherry trees in blossom, and clumps of heavily flowered rhododendrons filling in the odd corners; in the foreground you have a blaze of carnations or Shirley poppies, or tiger lilies in full bloom. As soon as the lunch is over and your guests have departed the garden departs also, and all the cats in Christendom can sit in council in your yard without causing you a moment's anxiety. If you have a bishop or an antiquary or something of that sort coming to lunch you just mention the fact when you are ordering the garden, and you get an old world pleasaunce, with clipped yew hedges and sundial and hollyhocks, and perhaps a mulberry tree, and borders of sweet williams and Canterbury bells, and an old-fashioned beehive or two tucked away in a corner. Those are the ordinary lines of supply that the Oasis Association undertakes, but by paying a few guineas a year extra you are entitled to its emergency E.O.N. service."

"What on earth is an E.O.N. service?"

"It's just like a conventional signal to indicate special cases like the incursion of Gwenda Pottingdon. It means you've got someone coming to lunch or dinner whose garden is alleged to be the 'the envy of the neighborhood.'"

"Yes," exclaimed Elinor, with some excitement, "and what happens then?"

"Something that sounds like a miracle out of the Arabian Nights. Your backyard becomes voluptuous with pomegranate and almond trees, lemon groves, and hedges of flowering cactus, dazzling banks of azaleas, marble-basined fountains, in which chestnut-and-white pond-herons step daintily amid exotic water lilies, while golden pheasants strut about on alabaster terraces. The whole effect rather suggests the idea that Providence and Norman Wilkinson have dropped mutual jealousies and collaborated to produce a background for an open air Russian Ballet; in point of fact, it is merely the background to your luncheon party. If there is any kick left in Gwenda Pottingdon, or whoever your E.O.N. guest of the moment may be, just mention carelessly that your climbing putella is the only one in England, since the one at Chatsworth died last winter. There isn't such a thing as a climbing putella, but Gwenda Pottingdon and her kind don't usually know one flower from another without prompting."

"Quick," said Elinor, "the address of the Association."

Gwenda Pottingdon did not enjoy her lunch. It was a simple yet elegant meal, excellently cooked and daintily served, but the piquant sauce of her own conversation was notably lacking. She had prepared a long succession of eulogistic comments on the wonders of her town garden, with its unrivaled effects of horticultural magnificence, and, behold, her theme was shut in on every side by the luxuriant hedge of Siberian berberis that formed a glowing background to Elinor's bewildering fragment of fairyland. The pomegranate and lemon trees, the terraced fountain, where gold carp slithered and wriggled amid the roots of gorgeous-hued irises, the banked masses of exotic blooms, the pagoda-like enclosure, where Japanese sandbadgers disported themselves, all these contributed to take away Gwenda's appetite and moderate her desire to talk about gardening matters.

"I can't say I admire the climbing putella," she observed shortly, "and anyway it's not the only one of its kind in England; I happen to know of one in Hampshire. How gardening is going out of fashion. I suppose people haven't the time for it nowadays."

Altogether it was quite one of Elinor's most successful luncheon parties.

It was distinctly an unforeseen catastrophe that Gwenda should have burst in on the household four days later at lunch-time and made her way unbidden into the dining room.

"I thought I must tell you that my Elaine has had a watercolor sketch accepted by the Latent Talent Art Guild; it's to be exhibited at their summer exhibition at the Hackney Gallery. It will be the sensation of the moment in the art world—Hullo, what on earth has happened to your garden? It's not there!"

"Suffragettes," said Elinor promptly; "didn't you hear about it? They broke in and made hay of the whole thing in about ten minutes. I was so heartbroken at the havoc that I had the whole place cleared out; I shall have it laid out again on rather more elaborate lines."

"That," she said to the Baroness afterwards, "is what I call having an emergency brain."

{ NASTURTIUM }

CYNTHIA ZARIN

Baby's Breath

No one could have expected it—least
of all me—which plant in the garden
    would grow the longest

tap root. "I'll just be a minute,"
I said, and stood the shovel in
    the ground, standing on it

like a stepladder, in the maple's
surge of new painted leaves. I stove
    and dug. I left off the shovel

and with my hands began to pry
the thing up from the dirt. Five
    fingers clutched me back. Dry

scrapings gripped the ivy. And then
I remembered its name, *Gypsophila,*
    and thought of the children

grabbing my sleeve on the Ponte Sisto,
their bright rags like the regalia
    of leaves now dropped into

the garden, grasping and pulling
until I felt we would all fall
        together, drowned, mewling

into the Tiber, back through silt,
through bitumen, to the heart's burial
        in the earth, dense milk

white breath rising like clouds or
stars in the cold Roman air—
        like clouds, or like flowers.

SARAH ORNE JEWETT

Mrs. Todd

Later, there was only one fault to find with this choice of a summer lodging-place, and that was its complete lack of seclusion. At first the tiny house of Mrs. Almira Todd, which stood with its end to the street, appeared to be retired and sheltered enough from the busy world, behind its bushy bit of a green garden, in which all the blooming things, two or three gay hollyhocks and some London-pride, were pushed back against the gray-shingled wall. It was a queer little garden and puzzling to a stranger, the few flowers being put at a disadvantage by so much greenery; but the discovery was soon made that Mrs. Todd was an ardent lover of herbs, both wild and tame, and the sea-breezes blew into the low end-window house laden with not only sweet-brier and sweet-mary, but balm and sage and borage and mint, wormwood and southernwood. If Mrs. Todd had occasion to step into the far corner of her herb plot, she trod heavily upon thyme, and made its fragrant presence known with all the rest. Being a very large person, her full skirts brushed and bent almost every slender stalk that her feet missed. You could always tell when she was stepping about there, even when you were half awake in the morning, and learned to know, in the course of a few weeks' experience, in exactly which corner of the garden she might be.

At one side of this herb plot were other growths of a rustic pharmacopœia, great treasures and rarities among the commoner herbs. There were some strange and pungent odors that roused a dim sense and remembrance of something in the forgotten past. Some of these might once have belonged to sacred and mystic rites, and have had some occult knowledge handed with them down the centuries; but now they pertained only to humble compounds brewed at intervals with molasses or vinegar or spirits in a small cauldron on Mrs. Todd's kitchen stove. They were dispensed to suffering neighbors, who usually came at night as if by stealth, bringing their own ancient-looking vials to be filled. One nostrum was called the Indian remedy, and its price was but fifteen cents; the whispered directions could be heard as customers passed the windows. With most remedies the purchaser was allowed to depart unadmonished from the kitchen, Mrs. Todd being a wise saver of steps; but with certain vials she gave cautions, standing in the doorway, and there were other doses which had to be accompanied on their healing way as far as the gate, while she muttered long chapters of directions, and kept up an air of secrecy and importance to the last. It may not have been only the common ails of humanity with which she tried to cope; it seemed sometimes as if love and hate and jealousy and adverse winds at sea might also find their proper remedies among the curious wild-looking plants in Mrs. Todd's garden.

The village doctor and this learned herbalist were upon the best of terms. The good man may have counted upon the unfavorable effect of certain potions which he should find his opportunity in counteracting; at any rate, he now and then stopped and exchanged greetings with Mrs. Todd over the picket fence. The conversation became at once professional after the briefest preliminaries, and he would stand twirling a sweet-scented sprig in his fingers, and make suggestive jokes, perhaps about her faith in a too persistent course of thoroughwort elixir, in which my landlady professed such firm belief as sometimes to endanger the life and usefulness of worthy neighbors.

To arrive at this quietest of seaside villages late in June, when the busy herb-gathering season was just beginning, was also to arrive in the early prime of Mrs. Todd's activity in the brewing of old-fashioned spruce beer. This cooling and refreshing drink had been brought to wonderful perfection through a long series of experiments; it had won immense local fame, and the supplies for its manufacture were always giving out and having to be replenished. For various reasons, the seclusion and uninterrupted days which had been looked forward to proved to be very rare in this otherwise delightful corner of the world. My hostess and I had made our shrewd business agreement on the basis of a simple cold luncheon at noon, and liberal restitution in the matter of hot suppers, to provide for which the lodger might sometimes be seen hurrying down the road, late in the day, with cunner line in hand. It was soon found that this arrangement made large allowance for Mrs. Todd's slow herb-gathering progresses through woods and pastures. The spruce-beer customers were pretty steady in hot weather, and there were many demands for different soothing syrups and elixirs with which the unwise curiosity of my early residence had made me acquainted. Knowing Mrs. Todd to be a widow, who had little beside this slender business and the income from one hungry lodger to maintain her, one's energies and even interest were quickly bestowed, until it became a matter of course that she should go afield every pleasant day, and that the lodger should answer all peremptory knocks at the side door.

In taking an occasional wisdom-giving stroll in Mrs. Todd's company, and in acting as business partner during her frequent absences, I found the July days fly fast, and it was not until I felt myself confronted with too great pride and pleasure in the display, one night, of two dollars and twenty-seven cents which I had taken in during the day, that I remembered a long piece of writing, sadly belated now, which I was bound to do. To have been patted kindly on the shoulder and called "darlin'," to have been offered a surprise of early mushrooms for supper, to have had all the glory of making two dollars and twenty-seven cents in a single day, and then to renounce it all and withdraw from these pleasant successes, needed much resolution. Literary employments are so vexed with uncertainties at best, and it was not until the voice of conscience sounded louder in my ears than the sea on the nearest pebble beach that I said unkind words of withdrawal to Mrs. Todd. She only became more wistfully affectionate than ever in her expressions, and looked as disappointed as I expected when I frankly told her that I could no longer enjoy the pleasure of what we called "seein' folks." I felt that I was cruel to a whole neighborhood in curtailing her liberty in this most important season for harvesting the different wild herbs that were so much counted upon to case their winter ails.

"Well, dear," she said sorrowfully, "I've took great advantage o' your bein' here. I ain't had such a season for years, but I have never had nobody I could so trust. All you lack is a few qualities, but with time you'd gain judgment an' experience, an' be very able in the business. I'd stand right here an' say it to anybody."

Mrs. Todd and I were not separated or estranged by the change in our business relations; on the contrary, a deeper intimacy seemed to begin. I do not know what herb of the night it was that used sometimes to send out a penetrating odor late in the evening, after the dew had fallen, and the moon was high, and the cool air came up from the sea. Then Mrs. Todd would feel that she must talk to somebody, and I was only too glad to listen. We both fell under the spell, and she either stood outside the window, or made an errand to my sitting-room, and told, it might be very commonplace news of the day, or, as happened one misty summer night, all that lay deepest in her heart. It was in this way that I came to know that she had loved one who was far above her.

"No, dear, him I speak of could never think of me," she said. "When we was young together his mother did n't favor the match, an' done everything she could to part us; and folks thought we both married well, but 't wa'n't' what either one of us wanted most; an' now we're left alone again, an' might have had each other all the time. He was above bein' a seafarin' man, an' prospered more than most; he come of a high family, an' my lot was plain an' hard-workin'. I ain't seen him for some years; he's forgot our youthful feelin's, I expect, but a woman's heart is different; them feelin's comes back when you think you've done with 'em, as sure as spring comes with the year. An' I've always had ways of hearin' about him."

She stood in the centre of a braided rug, and its rings of black and gray seemed to circle about her feet in the dim light. Her height and massiveness in the low room gave her the look of a huge sibyl, while the strange fragrance of the mysterious herb blew in from the little garden.

{ CANNA 'CLEOPATRA' }

WILLIAM CARLOS WILLIAMS

The Lily

The branching head of
tiger-lilies through the window
in the air—

A humming bird
is still on whirring wings
above the flowers—

By spotted petals curling back
and tongues that hang
the air is seen—

It's raining—
water's caught
among the curled-back petals

Caught and held
and there's a fly—
are blossoming

ARTURO VIVANTE

Fisherman's Terrace

. . . I remember a terrace on a steep and rocky slope over-
looking the sea. I came to it by chance one day early in
October two years ago, after I had driven with my wife from
Rome to Porto Santo Stefano, a small seaport on the north
side of the Monte Argentario, the promontory on the coast
of Tuscany, between Leghorn and Rome. The road that
connects the mainland to this little town continues beyond
it for a few miles, climbing steeply up the mountain but
keeping always in sight of the sea. It is a new road, and they
call it *"strada panoramica,"* scenic route. Someday it will
follow the sea along to Porto Ercole, a small harbor on the
south side of the mountain, and so complete the ring
around the promontory, but for now, owing to lack of
funds, it ends abruptly high above the shore, several miles
short of its goal. I drove to the end of it the morning after
we arrived in Porto Santo Stefano. My wife, who was con-
valescing, had stayed behind in the hotel.

There were no houses in sight, and, except for a field just below the road, the slope of the mountain all the way down to the sea, about a mile away, looked wild and untouched. I started to walk down. It was one of those clear October days on which one can't feel sad that the summer has ended — the mountain shone above me, and the sea below me; the grass I brushed through also shone, being light and dry, having lost all of its greenness, and being smooth and moved by the wind. On the field, ripe little tomatoes, too small for the farmer to bother with, shone here and there. I picked one and sucked its juice, and it was so tasty I picked another two. Farther down were some rows of vines. Their leaves were turning crimson. Some were crisp and brittle round the edges, others were still soft and green. The grapes had all been gathered, except at one corner of the vineyard, where I was surprised to find a vine from which several large, conspicuous bunches still hung. Though of a white variety, the grapes were so ripe that they looked almost red, and matched some of the colors of the leaves about them. I thought that perhaps they had been left on the plant to make some special wine, and I refrained from picking any.

The slope got steep and wild. I had to open a way with my arms through thick bushes of mountain laurel, or hunch up and walk backward through the brambles. Soon the bushes were so tall and thick I was quite hidden, and couldn't see the sun or the mountain or the sea. The ground was carpeted by moss, and I sat down. Sitting under that roof of foliage, in the silence of that wide green chamber, I felt as though I had disappeared, or sunk into oblivion, and that to find myself again I had to rise and go on. Almost regretfully, I did so. Suddenly a thin blacksnake glistened like a streak of oil on the ground in front of me and slid up the incline, a wonder of locomotion. Instantly, I became more alert; I picked up a stick and, slashing it about in front of me to scare away any more snakes that might lie on my path, I went on through the bushes, impatient to come to the end of them. Finding that the slope tended to be clearer on my left, I went that way along a horizontal shelf until I reached a creek. The water trickled down, almost hidden in the furrow it had created. It made a straight and smooth, if steep, path to the sea. I followed this, jumping down small, muddy waterfalls until I came to one that was too high to jump, and here, as I made a little detour to the right around the creek, I found myself among orange trees upon a terrace. It was a narrow shelf of level ground cleared of all bushes and carved into the slope. A stone wall supported it from below. Between the trees, some rocks too large to be removed rose from the ground like keels and prows. Besides the oranges, there were lemons, pomegranates set against the slope, a palm, a few olive trees, prickly pears, and, scattered here and there among the weeds, some hardy garden flowers—chrysanthemums in bloom, and amaranths. The oranges were still green, but the lemons were ripe, and the pomegranates were so ripe that some had fallen on the ground, and those that were still on their branches showed deep cracks. One was split open

and had shed some of its seeds; a few of these lay—
brown instead of crimson—straight below it. I picked a
pomegranate, broke it, and bit into a cell of succulent
and pulpy seeds. I wondered whose this terrace could
be. And why the unpicked fruit? Was it forsaken? Were
pomegranates worthless on the market? But what about
the lemons? They were ripe. And those flowers—did
they grow from seed, year after year?

With these questions in my mind, I followed a
barely traceable zigzag path to the sea, which was only
about a hundred feet down from the terrace. The creek
formed a sandy inlet in the rocky shore. Its trickle of
water was enough to keep the terrace fresh, its sand
enough for a rowboat to land on safely, and I thought
that a fisherman or a sailor with an inward longing for
land had eyed the creek and the narrow shelf beside it,
and built the terrace and planted fruit trees there.
Certainly it was much more accessible from the sea than
overland. Soon, I thought, perhaps in a few days, he will
row over from Porto Santo Stefano in a little boat, land
at the inlet, and climb up to his terrace with a basket. I
could almost see him—an old man wearing a beret and
blue jeans, tired of being tossed around by waves and
stormy weather.

I returned to the terrace, picked another pomegranate, put it in my pocket, and then began to climb back
up the slope along the creek. During rainstorms, it must
become a wild and roaring torrent, but now it came
down drop by drop and I found no pool deep enough to
drink clear water from. The water became muddy at the

27

slightest touch. When I saw the vineyard—way to my left—I was too thirsty to consider the special wine the farmer might have had in mind for the grapes left on the single vine, and I went over to them. I picked the rosiest-looking and ate them not with my fingers but thirstily, by holding the bunch against my mouth and biting into it as though it were an apple. It was sweet almost to excess, having had more than the usual time in which to ripen, and having drawn from earth and sun and air all the flavor they could give. I threw the bare bunch of stems into the air and picked another cluster. Not as thirsty now, I walked up the incline holding it in my hand and plucking the grapes slowly, one by one. I hadn't gone far when I saw an old man with a hoe coming toward me. He wore a shirt whose color, bleached by the sun, had faded to a light and rosy hue—similar to that of the grapes that I was eating. His trousers were the color of dry earth. He certainly looked as if he belonged here, and I felt timid with my stolen grapes.

He walked slowly, looking at the ground, and I thought I had better say something before he did. "I picked this bunch of grapes down there," I said, pointing at the corner of the vineyard. "There's a vine that still has all its grapes."

He nodded. "That's all right," he said, and from the way he spoke—with a kind smile—I knew that he wouldn't have said anything about the bunch of grapes.

"Why wasn't that vine picked?" I asked him.

He brought the hoe down from his shoulder to the ground and rested on it. "We always leave one vine unpicked," he said. "For the stranger. It is an ancient custom."

"Oh," I said.

"Yes, it's supposed to bring us luck for the next season."

"Well, I hope this brings you luck—here I am, a stranger," I said, raising the grapes as though they were already wine and I were toasting.

"Yes," he said, and he repeated, almost apologetically, "it is an ancient custom."

"I went all the way down to the sea," I said. "Whose is that terrace near the mouth of the creek with oranges, lemons, and pomegranates—all unpicked?"

"Oh, you've been down there," he said. "A fisherman from Porto Santo Stefano planted those trees when there was no road up here and all this slope was wild. He didn't buy the land, though. Until this road was built, nobody cared. But the value of land now has risen, and the owner here told him that it wasn't his."

"Not his?" I said. "And no one picks the fruit?"

"No," he replied. "It's too far down the slope for a few trees. *He* used to go there by boat, of course. It was all right for him."

I left the farmer and went up the slope, wishing I could buy the terrace and give it to the fisherman. I thought of him, of his carefully choosing the land near the mouth of the creek, of his clearing the bushes away and digging up all the rocks that weren't too deep-set and massive to be removed, of his building the supporting wall and planting the trees and the flowers, and then, when the trees had begun bearing fruit, being told to go. I pictured the man who had bought the land—probably some big-paunched contractor from Rome or Grosseto, who had got it from the government for very little. I had an idea it would be sold in lots as Porto Santo Stefano expanded and that coast became more and more fashionable. Already there were new little villas a mile or two from the town, and others were rising just around the corner from here. One could be sure that in a few years this uninhabited slope would have its own gleaming white little houses, and a serpentine road running all the way down to the sea. The fisherman, I was thinking, should have gone farther, around the next point, where perhaps he could have come to the end of his years undisturbed. Or had all this coast become so valuable that there was no ledge from which he wouldn't be ousted? Perhaps it was so, and he should have stuck to fishing and the sea, which belonged to no man and every man, and off which only stormy weather could sweep him.

With these thoughts in mind, I drove back to Porto Santo Stefano. Once or twice, as I thought of the terrace, I wished I could buy it for myself, for it corresponded in every detail with what I desired—oranges were my favorite trees; it was on the sea and was backed by a high mountain whose name (Argentario) suggested to me rocks streaked with silver; since it looked west, there would be a view of the sun setting over the Island of Giglio or the sea, depending on the time of the year: it was on a promontory (an island with an avenue of escape, my favorite land formation), and it was in Tuscany, almost equidistant from Siena and Rome; it had a creek, a stone wall, an inlet; there were olive trees . . .

"Even if I could buy it, though," I said to myself, "I would feel like a trespasser, like a usurper—I would never be able to keep it."

That evening, strolling with my wife along the water-front of one of the two crescent-shaped harbors of the little town, I saw many fishermen, some sitting on benches, others talking to one another and standing in little circles opposite a fleet of moored fishing boats and in between mounds of brown nets. I approached one who was alone, a dark and sinewy middle-aged man wearing a blue sweater and a beret tilted to cover most of his forehead. "Excuse me," I said to him. "A few miles around the coast, in the direction of Porto Ercole, I came to a little terrace on the sea with fruit trees on it. I wonder if you know who built it. I hear it was a fisher-man from here."

"That one," he said, pointing to a man who was sit-ting alone two benches over—a big, brawny man with hoary hair, wide lips, and a sullen look.

We went over to him. "That fisherman over there," I said, "told me that you built the terrace on the sea I saw this morning down from where the new road ends."

His face, which at first had seemed opaque to me, lightened in all its features. "Have you been up there?" he asked, speaking as one would who was used to approaching it from below.

"Yes," I said. "It's a fine terrace, and those are beautiful trees that you planted. But is it true that they won't let you pick them?"

"That land doesn't belong to me," he said.

"So I've heard," I said. "I think it's an injustice."

"Why?" he said. "It isn't my property. I went there thinking no one would ever care. I recognize I made a mistake."

"They should let you pick the fruit you planted."

He shrugged his shoulders.

"That terrace belongs to you more than to anybody else."

He shook his head and looked out toward the sea, his face impassive. Then he turned to me. "When you work land that isn't yours," he said, "that's what you have to expect." He continued looking at me, as though to see if I could reply.

I couldn't. I could only nod. In my pocket I still had the pomegranate I had picked. "This is from your terrace," I said, offering it to him.

"Give it to the signora," he said, looking at my wife. We thanked him and left.

"Surely," I said to my wife, "that land is his."

"He doesn't think so."

"But it's his, nonetheless—in a way altogether irrelevant to whoever has bought it."

"Irrelevant to him, too, I'm afraid."

"Oh, I don't know. I am sure he returns to it again and again in his thoughts—lands there, goes up and sits under a tree, gathers the fruit in his basket."

"I can see that *you* do," she said. "You are co-owners."

{ FRITILLARIA PERSICA }

JAMES SCHUYLER

What Ails My Fern?

My peonies have lovely leaves
but rarely flower.
Oh, they have buds
and plenty of them. These
grow to the size of peas
and stay
that way.
Is this
bud blast?

What ails my fern?

I enclose a sample
of a white disease
on a leaf
of honesty
known also
as the money plant

My two blue spruce
look worse and worse

What ails my fern?

Two years ago a tenant
wound tape around my tree.
Sap dripped out of the branches
on babies in buggies below. So
I unwound the tape.
Can nothing be done
to revive my tree?

What ails my fern?

I hate my disordered
backyard fence
where lilac, weigela
and mock orange grow.
Please advise
how to get rid of it.

Weeping willow roots
reaching out
seeking water
fill my cesspool and well.
What do you suggest?

What ails my fern?

WILLIAM SAROYAN

The Pomegranate Trees

My uncle Melik was just about the worst farmer that ever lived. He was too imaginative and poetic for his own good. What he wanted was beauty. He wanted to plant it and see it grow. I myself planted over one hundred pomegranate trees for my uncle one year back there in the good old days of poetry and youth in the world. I drove a John Deere tractor too, and so did my uncle. It was all pure esthetics, not agriculture. My uncle just liked the idea of planting trees and watching them grow.

Only they wouldn't grow. It was on account of the soil. The soil was desert soil. It was dry. My uncle waved at the six hundred and eighty acres of desert he had bought and he said in the most poetic Armenian anybody ever heard, Here in this awful desolation a garden shall flower, fountains of cold water shall bubble out of the earth, and all things of beauty shall come into being.

Yes, sir, I said.

I was the first and only relative to see the land he had bought. He knew I was a poet at heart, and he believed I would understand the magnificent impulse that was driving him to glorious ruin. I did. I knew as well as he that what he had purchased was worthless desert land. It was away over to hell and gone, at the foot of the Sierra Nevada Mountains. It was full of every kind of desert plant that ever sprang out of dry hot earth. It was overrun with prairie dogs, squirrels, horned toads, snakes, and a variety of smaller forms of life. The space over this land knew only the presence of hawks, eagles, and buzzards. It was a region of loneliness, emptiness, truth, and dignity. It was nature at its proudest, dryest, loneliest, and loveliest.

My uncle and I got out of the Ford roadster in the middle of his land and began to walk over the dry earth.

This land, he said, is my land.

He walked slowly, kicking into the dry soil. A horned toad scrambled over the earth at my uncle's feet. My uncle clutched my shoulder and came to a pious halt.

What is that animal? he said.

That little tiny lizard? I said.

That mouse with horns, my uncle said. What is it?

I don't know for sure, I said. We call them horny toads.

The horned toad came to a halt about three feet away and turned its head.

My uncle looked down at the small animal.

Is it poison? he said.

To eat? I said. Or if it bites you?

Either way, my uncle said.

I don't think it's good to eat, I said. I think it's harmless. I've caught many of them. They grow sad in captivity, but never bite. Shall I catch this one?

Please do, my uncle said.

I sneaked up on the horned toad, then sprang on it while my uncle looked on.

Careful, he said. Are you sure it isn't poison?

I've caught many of them, I said.

I took the horned toad to my uncle. He tried not to seem afraid.

A lovely little thing, isn't it? he said. His voice was unsteady.

Would you like to hold it? I said.

No, my uncle said. You hold it. I have never before been so close to such a thing as this. I see it has eyes. I suppose it can see us.

I suppose it can, I said. It's looking up at you now.

My uncle looked the horned toad straight in the eye. The horned toad looked my uncle straight in the eye. For fully half a minute they looked one another straight in the eye and then the horned toad turned its head aside and looked down at the ground. My uncle sighed with relief.

A thousand of them, he said, could kill a man, I suppose.

They never travel in great numbers, I said. You hardly ever see more than one at a time.

A big one, my uncle said, could probably bite a man to death.

39

They don't grow big, I said. This is as big as they grow.

They seem to have an awful eye for such small creatures, my uncle said. Are you sure they don't mind being picked up?

I suppose they forget all about it the minute you put them down, I said.

Do you really think so? my uncle said.

I don't think they have very good memories, I said.

My uncle straightened up, breathing deeply.

Put the little creature down, he said. Let us not be cruel to the innocent creations of Almighty God. If it is not poison and grows no larger than a mouse and does not travel in great numbers and has no memory to speak of, let the timid little thing return to the earth. Let us be gentle toward these small things which live on the earth with us.

Yes sir, I said.

I placed the horned toad on the ground.

Gently now, my uncle said. Let no harm come to this strange dweller on my land.

The horned toad scrambled away.

These little things, I said, have been living on soil of this kind for centuries.

Centuries? my uncle said. Are you sure?

I'm not sure, I said, but I imagine they have. They're still here, anyway.

My uncle looked around at his land, at the cactus and brush growing out of it, at the sky overhead.

What have they been eating all this time? he shouted.

I don't know, I said.

What would you say they've been eating? he said.

Insects, I guess.

Insects? my uncle shouted. What sort of insects?

Little bugs, most likely, I said. I don't know their names. I can find out tomorrow at school.

We continued to walk over the dry land. When we came to some holes in the earth my uncle stood over them and said, What lives down there?

Prairie dogs, I said.

What are *they*? he said.

Well, I said, they're something like rats. They belong to the rodent family.

What are all these things doing on my land? my uncle said.

They don't know it's your land, I said. They've been living here a long while.

I don't suppose that horny toad ever looked a man in the eye before, my uncle said.

I don't think so, I said.

Do you think I scared it or anything? my uncle said.

I don't know for sure, I said.

If I did, my uncle said, I didn't mean to. I'm going to build a house here some day.

I didn't know that, I said.

Of course, my uncle said. I'm going to build a magnificent house.

It's pretty far away, I said.

It's only an hour from town, my uncle said.

If you go fifty miles an hour, I said.

It's not fifty miles to town, my uncle said. It's thirty-seven.

Well, you've got to take a little time out for rough roads, I said.

I'll build me the finest house in the world, my uncle said. What else lives on this land?

Well, I said, there are three or four kinds of snakes.

Poison or non-poison? my uncle said.

Mostly non-poison, I said. The rattlesnake is poison, though.

Do you mean to tell me there are *rattlesnakes* on this land? my uncle said.

This is the kind of land rattlesnakes usually live on, I said.

How many? my uncle said.

Per acre? I said. Or on the whole six hundred and eighty acres?

Per acre, my uncle said.

Well, I said, I'd say there are about three per acre, conservatively.

Three per acre? my uncle shouted. Conservatively?

Maybe only two, I said.

How many is that to the whole place? my uncle said.

Well, let's see, I said. Two per acre. Six hundred and eighty acres. About fifteen hundred of them.

Fifteen hundred of them? my uncle said.

An acre is pretty big, I said. Two rattlesnakes per acre isn't many. You don't often see them.

What else have we got around here that's poison? my uncle said.

I don't know of anything else, I said. All the other things are harmless. The rattlesnakes are pretty harmless too, unless you step on them.

All right, my uncle said. You walk ahead and watch where you're going. If you see a rattlesnake, don't step on it. I don't want you to die at the age of eleven.

Yes, sir, I said. I'll watch carefully.

We turned around and walked back to the Ford. I didn't see any rattlesnakes on the way back. We got into the car and my uncle lighted a cigarette

I'm going to make a garden of the awful desolation, he said.

Yes, sir, I said.

I know what my problems are, my uncle said, and I know how to solve them.

How? I said.

Do you mean the horny toads or the rattlesnakes? my uncle said.

I mean the problems, I said.

Well, my uncle said, the first thing I'm going to do is hire some Mexicans and put them to work.

Doing what? I said.

Clearing the land, my uncle said. Then I'm going to have them dig for water.

Dig where? I said.

Straight down, my uncle said. After we get water, I'm going to have them plow the land and then I'm going to plant.

What are you going to plant? I said. Wheat?

Wheat? my uncle shouted. What do I want with wheat? Bread is five cents a loaf. I'm going to plant pomegranate trees.

How much are pomegranates? I said.

Pomegranates, my uncle said, are practically unknown in this country.

Is that all you're going to plant? I said.

I have in mind, my uncle said, planting several other kinds of trees.

Peach trees? I said.

About ten acres, my uncle said.

How about apricots? I said.

By all means, my uncle said. The apricot is a lovely fruit. Lovely in shape, with a glorious flavor and a most delightful pit. I shall plant about twenty acres of apricot trees.

I hope the Mexicans don't have any trouble finding water, I said. Is there water under this land?

Of course, my uncle said. The important thing is to get started. I shall instruct the men to watch our for rattlesnakes. Pomegranates, he said. Peaches. Apricots. What else?

Figs? I said.

Thirty acres of figs, my uncle said.

How about mulberries? I said. The mulberry tree is a very nice-looking tree.

Mulberries, my uncle said. He moved his tongue around in his mouth. A nice tree, he said. A tree I knew well in the old country. How many acres would you suggest?

About ten, I said.

All right, he said. What else?

Olive trees are nice, I said.

Yes, they are, my uncle said. One of the nicest. About ten acres of olive trees. What else?

Well, I said, I don't suppose apple trees would grow on this kind of land.

I suppose not, my uncle said. I don't like apples anyway.

He started the car and we drove off the dry land on to the dry road. The car bounced about slowly until we reached the road and then we began to travel at a higher rate of speed.

One thing, my uncle said. When we get home I would rather you didn't mention this *farm* to the folks.

Yes, sir, I said. (*Farm?* I thought. *What farm?*)

I want to surprise them, my uncle said. You know how your grandmother is. I'll go ahead with my plans and when everything is in order I'll take the whole family out to the farm and surprise them.

Yes, sir, I said.

Not a word to a living soul, my uncle said.

Yes, sir, I said.

Well, the Mexicans went to work and cleared the land. They cleared about ten acres of it in about two months. There were seven of them. They worked with shovels and hoes. They didn't understand anything about anything. It all seemed very strange, but they never complained. They were being paid and that was the thing that counted. They were two brothers and their sons. One day the older brother, Diego, very politely asked my uncle what it was they were supposed to be doing.

Señor, he said, please forgive me. Why are we cutting down the cactus?

I'm going to farm this land, my uncle said.

The other Mexicans asked Diego in Mexican what my uncle had said and Diego told them.

They didn't believe it was worth the trouble to tell my uncle he couldn't do it. They just went on cutting down the cactus.

The cactus, however, stayed down only for a short while. The land which had been first cleared was already rich again with fresh cactus and brush. My uncle made this observation with considerable amazement.

It takes deep plowing to get rid of cactus, I said. You've got to plow it out.

My uncle talked the matter over with Ryan, who had a farm-implement business. Ryan told him not to fool with horses. The modern thing to do was to turn a good tractor loose on the land and do a year's work in a day.

So my uncle bought a John Deere tractor. It was beautiful. A mechanic from Ryan's taught Diego how to operate the tractor, and the next day when my uncle and I reached the land we could see the tractor away out in the desolation and we could hear it booming in the awful emptiness of the desert. It sounded pretty awful. It *was* awful. My uncle thought it was wonderful.

Progress, he said. There's the modern age for you.

Ten thousand years ago, he said, it would have taken a hundred men a week to do what the tractor's done today.

Ten thousand years ago? I said. You mean yesterday.

Anyway, my uncle said, there's nothing like these modern conveniences.

The tractor isn't a convenience, I said.

What is it, then? my uncle said. Doesn't the driver sit?

He couldn't very well stand, I said.

Any time they let you sit, my uncle said, it's a convenience. Can you whistle?

Yes, sir, I said. What sort of a song would you like to hear?

Song? my uncle said. I don't want to hear any song. I want you to whistle at that Mexican on the tractor.

What for? I said.

Never mind what for, my uncle said. Just whistle. I want him to know we are here and that we are pleased with his work. He's probably plowed twenty acres.

Yes, sir, I said.

I put the second and third fingers of each hand into my mouth and blew with all my might. It was good and loud. Nevertheless, it didn't seem as if Diego had heard me. He was pretty far away. We were walking toward him anyway, so I couldn't figure out why my uncle wanted me to whistle at him.

Once again, he said.

I whistled once again, but Diego didn't hear.

Louder, my uncle said.

This next time I gave it all I had, and my uncle put his hands over his ears. My face got very red, too. The Mexican on the tractor heard the whistle this time. He slowed the tractor down, turned it around, and began plowing straight across the field toward us.

Do you want him to do that? I said.

It doesn't matter, my uncle said.

In less than a minute and a half the tractor and the Mexican arrived. The Mexican seemed very delighted. He wiped dirt and perspiration off his face and got down from the tractor.

Señor, he said, this is wonderful.

I'm glad you like it, my uncle said.

Would you like a ride? the Mexican asked my uncle.

My uncle didn't know for sure. He looked at me.

Go ahead, he said. Hop on. Have a little ride.

Diego got on the tractor and helped me on. He sat on the metal seat and I stood behind him, holding him. The tractor began to shake, then jumped, and then began to move. It moved swiftly and made a good deal of noise. The Mexican drove around in a big circle and brought the tractor back to my uncle. I jumped off.

All right, my uncle said to the Mexican. Go back to your work.

The Mexican drove the tractor back to where he was plowing.

My uncle didn't get water out of the land until many months later. He had wells dug all over the place, but no water came out of the wells. Of course he had motor pumps too, but even then no water came out. A water specialist named Roy came out from Texas with his two younger brothers and they began investigating the land. They told my uncle they'd get water for him. It took them three months and the water was muddy and there wasn't much of it. There was a trickle of muddy water. The specialist told my uncle matters would improve with time and went back to Texas.

Now half the land was cleared and plowed and there was water, so the time had come to plant.

We planted pomegranate trees. They were of the finest quality and very expensive. We planted about seven hundred of them. I myself planted a hundred. My uncle planted quite a few. We had a twenty-acre orchard of pomegranate trees away over to hell and gone in the strangest desolation anybody ever saw. It was the loveliest-looking absurdity imaginable and my uncle was crazy about it. The only trouble was, his money was giving out. Instead of going ahead and trying to make a garden of the whole six hundred and eighty acres, he decided to devote all his time and energy and money to the pomegranate trees.

Only for the time being, he said. Until we begin to market the pomegranates and get our money back.

Yes, sir, I said.

I didn't know for sure, but I figured we wouldn't be getting any pomegranates to speak of off those little trees for two or three years at least, but I didn't say anything. My uncle got rid of the Mexican workers and he and I took over the farm. We had the tractor and a lot of land, so every now and then we drove out to the farm and drove the tractor around, plowing up cactus and turning over the soil between the pomegranate trees. This went on for three years.

One of these days, my uncle said, you'll see the loveliest garden in the world in this desert.

The water situation didn't improve with time, either. Every once in a while there would be a sudden generous spurt of water containing only a few pebbles and my uncle would be greatly pleased, but the next day it would be muddy again and there would be only a little trickle. The pomegranate trees fought bravely for life, but they never did get enough water to come out with any fruit.

There were blossoms after the fourth year. This was a great triumph for my uncle. He went out of his head with joy when he saw them.

Nothing much ever came of the blossoms, though. They were very beautiful, but that was about all. Purple and lonely.

That year my uncle harvested three small pomegranates.

I ate one, he ate one, and we kept the other one up in his office.

The following year I was fifteen. A lot of wonderful things had happened to me. I mean, I had read a number of good writers and I'd grown as tall as my uncle. The farm was still our secret. It had cost my uncle a lot of money, but he was always under the impression that very soon he was going to start marketing his pomegranates and get his money back and go on with his plan to make a garden in the desert.

The trees didn't fare very well. They grew a little, but it was hardly noticeable. Quite a few of them withered and died.

That's average, my uncle said. Twenty trees to an acre is only average. We won't plant new trees just now. We'll do that later.

He was still paying for the land, too.

The following year he harvested about two hundred pomegranates. He and I did the harvesting. They were pretty sad-looking pomegranates. We packed them in nice-looking boxes and my uncle shipped them to a wholesale produce house in Chicago. There were eleven boxes.

We didn't hear from the wholesale produce house for a month, so one night my uncle made a long-distance phone call. The produce man, D'Agostino, told my uncle nobody wanted pomegranates.

How much are you asking per box? my uncle shouted over the phone.

One dollar, D'Agostino shouted back.

That's not enough, my uncle shouted. I won't take a nickel less than five dollars a box.

They don't want them at one dollar a box, D'Agostino shouted.

Why not? my uncle shouted.

They don't know what they are, D'Agostino shouted.

What kind of a business man are you anyway? my

uncle shouted. They're pomegranates. I want five dollars a box.

I can't sell them, the produce man shouted. I ate one myself and I don't see anything so wonderful about them.

You're crazy, my uncle shouted. There is no other fruit in the world like the pomegranate. Five dollars a box isn't half enough.

What shall I do with them? D'Agostino shouted. I can't sell them. I don't want them.

I see, my uncle whispered. Ship them back. Ship them back express collect.

The phone call cost my uncle about seventeen dollars.

So the eleven boxes came back.

My uncle and I ate most of the pomegranates.

The following year my uncle couldn't make any more payments on the land. He gave the papers back to the man who had sold him the land. I was in the office at the time.

Mr. Griffith, my uncle said, I've got to give you back your property, but I would like to ask a little favor. I've planted twenty acres of pomegranate trees out there on that land and I'd appreciate it very much if you'd let me take care of those trees.

Take care of them? Mr. Griffith said. What in the world for?

My uncle tried to explain, but couldn't. It was too much to try to explain to a man who wasn't sympathetic.

So my uncle lost the land, and the trees, too.

About three years later he and I drove out to the

land and walked out to the pomegranate orchard. The trees were all dead. The soil was heavy again with cactus and desert brush. Except for the small dead pomegranate trees the place was exactly the way it had been all the years of the world.

We walked around in the orchard for a while and then went back to the car.

We got into the car and drove back to town.

We didn't say anything because there was such an awful lot to say, and no language to say it in.

{ CASTOR BEAN 'CARMENCITA' }

CHRISTOPHER REID

The Gardeners

I love these gardens, all their show
of antiquated art nouveau:
the buxom ironwork, candle-drips
and blobby leafage.
                              It is as if
someone had stumbled by surprise
on Alaodin's paradise.

It rains all evening—knives and forks.
The meteors drop by like corks.
Perpetuum mobile, a wind
hums in its box, as gardeners spend
endless, hermetic, twilight hours,
stooping above their hungry flowers.

This is the world's arcanest grove.
The borborygmus of a dove
calls from the belly of its bush.
How carefully the gardeners push
between the clumps of guzzling shrubs,
that line the way in wooden tubs.

With mashing faces, curled-up claws,
most of these blooms are carnivores.
Anyone sees, who wanders here,
a ruby clinging to an ear,
fat fingers, an outlandish wig . . .
The flowers grow slovenly and big,

as gardeners in white linen coats
rotate about their captious throats.
They have a god here, stern and jealous,
wearing four hats and five umbrellas,
who contemplates them, as they strive
to keep strange appetites alive.

MARY AUSTIN

Old Spanish Gardens

Dona Ina Manuelita Echivarra had come to the time of
life when waists were not to be mentioned. It took all
the evidence of her name to convince you that her cheek
had once known tints of the olive and apricot. Tio Juan,
who sunned himself daily in her patio, had achieved the
richness of weathered teak; his moustachios were
whitened as with the rime that collects on old adobes
sometimes near the sea-shore. But Dona Ina, who
missed by a score of years his mark of the days of
mañana por la mañana, was muddily dark, and her
moustache—but one does not suggest such things of a
lady, and that Dona Ina was a lady could be proved by a
foot so delicately arched and pointed, an ankle so neat
that there was not another like it in your acquaintance
save the mate to it.

Once you had seen it peeping forth from under the
black skirt—have not Castilian ladies worn black

immemorially?—you did not require the assurance of
Tio Juan that there was no one in her day could have
danced *la jota* with Dona Ina Manuelita.

She would clack the castanets for you occasionally
still, just to show how it was done, or with the guitar
resting on the arm of her chair—laps were no more to
be thought of than waists were—she would quaver a
song, *La Golindrina* for choice, or *La Noche esta
Serena*. But unquestionably Dona Ina's time had gone
by for shining at anything but conversation. She would
talk, and never so fruitfully as when the subject was her
garden.

A Spanish garden is a very intimate affair. It is the
innermost undergarment of the family life. Dona Ina's
was walled away from the world by six feet of adobe,
around the top of which still lingered the curved red
tiles of Mission manufacture. It was not spoken of as the
garden at all, it was the patio, an integral part of the
dwelling. There was, in fact, a raw hide cot on the long
gallery which gave access to it, and Dona Ina's drawn-
work chemises bleaching in the sun. The patio is a gift
to us from Andalusia; it is more Greek than Oriental,
and the English porch has about as much relation to it
as the buttons on the back of a man's coat to the sword-
belt they were once supposed to accommodate. The
patio is the original mud-walled enclosure of a people
who preferred living in the open but were driven to pro-
tection; the rooms about three sides of it were an after-
thought.

The Echivarra patio did not lack the indispensable

features of the early California establishment, the raised grill or cooking platform, and the ramada, the long vine-covered trellis where one took wine with one's friends, or the ladies of the family sat sewing at their interminable drawn work, *enramada*. The single vine which covered the twenty-foot trellis was of Mission stock, and had been planted by Dona Ina's father in the year the Pathfinder came over Tejon Pass into the great twin valleys. In Dona Ina's childhood a wine-press had stood in the corner of the patio where now there was a row of artichokes, which had been allowed to seed in order that their stiff silken tassels, dyed blue and crimson, might adorn the pair of china vases on either side the high altar. Dona Ina was nothing if not religious. In the corner of the patio farthest from the gallery, a fig-tree—this also is indispensable—hung over the tiled wall like a cloud. There was a weeping willow in the midst of the garden, and just outside, on either side of the door, two great pepper trees of the very stock of the parent of all pepper trees in Alta California, which a sea captain from South America gave to the Padre at San Luis Rey. Along the east wall there were pomegranates.

A pomegranate is the one thing that makes me understand what a pretty woman is to some men—the kind of prettiness that was Dona Ina's in the days when she danced *la jota*. The flower of the pomegranate has the crumpled scarlet of lips that find their excuse in simply being scarlet and folded like the petals of a flower; and then the fruit, warm from the sunny wall, faintly odorous, dusky flushed! It is so tempting when

61 ❧

broken open—that sort opens of its own accord if you leave it long enough on the bush—the rich heart colour, and the pleasant uncloying, sweet, sub-acid taste. One tastes and tastes—but when all is said and done there is nothing to a pomegranate except colour and flavour, and at least if it does not nourish neither does it give you indigestion. That is what suggests the comparison; there are so many people who would like to find a pretty woman in the same category. Always when we sat together nibbling the rosy seeds, I could believe, even without the evidence of the ankles, that Dona Ina had had her pomegranate days. Only, of course, she would not have smelled so of musk and—there is no denying it—of garlic. Thick-walled old adobes of the period of the Spanish Occupation give off a faint reek of this compelling condiment at every pore, and as for the musk, it was always about the gallery in saucers and broken flower-pots.

And yet Dona Ina was sensitive to odours: she told me that she had had the datura moved from the place where her mother had planted it, to the far end of the patio, where after nightfall its heavy, slightly fetid perfume, unnoticeable by day, scented all the air. She added that she felt convicted by this aversion of a want of sentiment toward a plant whose wide, papery-white bells went by the name of "Angels' trumpets."

On the day that she told me about the datura, which I had only recognized by its resemblance to its offensive wayside congener, the "jimson weed," the Señora Echivarra had been washing her hair with a tonic made of oil expressed from the seeds of the megharizza after a recipe which her mother had had from *her* mother, who had it from an Indian who used to peddle vegetables from the Mission, driving in every Saturday in an ancient caretta. I was interested to know if it were any more efficacious than the young shoots of the golden poppy fried in olive oil, which I had already tried. So we fell to talking of the virtues of plants and their application.

We began with the blessed "herb of the saints," dried bunches of which hung up under the rafters of the gallery as an unfailing resort in affections of the respiratory tract, and *yerba buena*, in which she was careful to distinguish between the creeping, aromatic *del campo* of the woodlands and the *yerba buena del poso*, "herb of the well," the common mint of damp places. When she added that the buckskin bag on the wall contained shavings of *cascara sagrada*, the sacred bark of the native buckthorn, indispensable to all nurseries, I knew that she had named two of the three most important contributions of the west to the modern pharmacopœia. This particular bag of bark had been sent from Sonoma County, for south of Monterey it grows too thin to be worth the gathering. The Grindelia, she told me, had come from the salt marshes about the mouth of the Pajaro, where Don Gaspar de Portola must have crossed going northward.

"And were you then at such pains to secure them?"

"In the old days, yes," she assured me. In her mother's time there was a regular traffic carried on by means of roving Indians in healing herbs and simples; things you could get now by no means whatever.

"As for instance—?" I was curious.

Well, there was creosote gum, which came from the desert beyond the Sierra Wall, valuable for sores and for rheumatism. It took me a moment or two, however, to recognise in her appellation of it (*hideondo*, stinking) the shiny, shellac-covered *larrea* of the arid regions. There were roots also of the holly-leaved barberry, which came from wet mountains northward, and of the "skunk cabbage," which were to be found only in soggy mountain meadows, where any early spring, almost before the frost was out of the ground, bears could be seen rooting it from the sod, fairly burying themselves in the black, peaty loam.

But when it came to *yerba mansa*, Dona Ina averred, her mother would trust nobody for its gathering. She would take an Indian or two and as many of her ten children as could not be trusted to be left at home, and make long *pasears* into the coast ranges for this succulent cure-all. I knew it well for one of the loveliest of meadow-haunting plants; wherever springs babbled, wherever a mountain stream lost itself under the roble oaks, the *yerba mansa* lifted above its heart-shaped leaves of pale green, quaint, winged cones on pink, pellucid stems. But I had never heard one half of the curative wonders which Dona Ina related of it. Efficacious in rheumatism, invaluable in pulmonary complaints, its bruised leaves reduced swellings, the roots were tonic and alterative.

I spare you the whole list, for Dona Ina was directly of the line of that lovely Señorita who had disdainfully described the English as the race who "pay for everything," and to her mind it took a whole category of virtues to induce so much effort as a trip into the mountains which had not a *baile* or a *fiesta* at the end of it. Other things that were sought for by the housewives of the Spanish Occupation were *amole*, or soaproot, the bulbs of a delicate, orchid-like lily which comes up in the late summer among the stems of the chaparral, and the roots of the wild gourd, the *chili-cojote*, a powerful purgative. Green fruit of this most common pest, said Dona Ina, pounded to a pulp, did wonders in the way of removing stains from clothing.

Then there was artemisia, romero, azalea, the blue-eyed grass of our meadows, upon an infusion of which fever patients can subsist for days, and elder, potent against spells, and there was Virgin's bower, which brought us back to the patio, for a great heap of it lay on the roof of the gallery, contesting the space there with the yellow banksia roses. I had supposed, until the Señora Echivarra mentioned it, that its purpose was purely ornamental, but I was to learn that it had come into the garden as *yerba de chivato* about the time the barbed-wire fences of the gringo began to make a remedy for cuts indispensable to the ranchero who valued the appearance of his live stock. When the eye, travelling along its twisty stems and twining leaf-stalks, came to a clump of yarrow growing at the root of it I began at once to suspect the whole garden. Was not the virtue of yarrow known even to the Greeks?

There was thyme flowering in the damp corner beyond the dripping faucet, and pot-marigold, lavender, rosemary, and lemon verbena, all plants that grow deep into the use and remembrance of man.

No friend of our race, not even the dog, has been more faithful. The stock of these had come overseas from Spain—were not the Phoenicians credited with introducing the pomegranate into Hispaniola?—and thence by way of the Missions.

All the borders of Dona Ina's garden were edged with rosy thrift, a European variety; and out on the headlands, a mile away, a paler, native cousin of it bloomed gaily with beach asters and yellow sand verbenas, but there was no one who knew by what winds, what communicating rootlets, they had exchanged greetings.

Observation, travelling by way of the borders, came to the datura, which was to set the conversation off again, this time not of plants curative, but hurtful. We knew of the stupefying effects of the bruised pods and roots of this species, and—this was my contribution—how the Paiute Indians used to administer the commoner variety, called *main-oph-weep*, to their warriors to produce the proper battle frenzy, and especially to young women about to undergo the annual ordeal of the "Dance of Marriageable Maidens."

Every year, at the spring gathering of the tribes, the maidens piled their dowries in a heap, and for three days, fasting, danced about it. If they fell or fainted, it was a sure sign they were not yet equal to the duties of housekeeping and childbearing; but I had had Paiute women tell me that they would never have endured the trial without a mild decoction of *main-oph-weep*.

"It was different with us," insisted Dona Ina; "many a time we have danced the sun up over the mountain, and been ready to begin again the next evening. . . . " But I wished to talk of the properties of plants, not of young ladies.

They mystery of poison plants oppressed me. One may understand how a scorpion stings in self-protection, but what profit has the "poison oak" of its virulence? It is not oak at all, but *Rhus trilobata*, and in the spring whole hillsides are enlivened by the shining bronze of its young foliage, or made crimson in September. But the pollen that floats from it in May in clouds, the sticky sap, or even the acrid smoke from the clearing where it is being exterminated, is an active poison to the human skin, though I had not heard that any animal suffered similarly. Dona Ina opined that there was never an evil plant let loose in the gardens of the Lord but the remedy was set to grow beside it. A wash of manzanita tea, Grindelia, or even buckthorn, she insisted, was excellent for poison oak. Best of all was a paste of pounded "soaproot." She knew a plant, too, which was corrective of the form of madness induced by the "loco" weed, whose pale foliage and delicately tinted, bladdery pods may be found always about the borders of the chaparral. For the convulsions caused by wild parsnip there was the wonder-working *yerba del pasmo*. This she knew also as a specific for snake-bite and tetanus. So greatly was it valued by mothers of fam-

ilies in the time of the Spanish Occupation, that when a
clearing was made for a house and patio, in any country
where it grew, a plant or two was always left standing.
But it was not until I had looked for it, where she said I
would find it between the oleander and the lemon verbena, that I recognised the common "grease-wood," the
chamise of the mesa country.

"But were there no plants, Dona Ina, which had
another meaning, flowers of affection, corrective to the
spirit?"

"Angelica," she considered doubtfully. Young
maids, on occasions of indecision, would pin a sprig of
it across their bosoms, she said, and after they had been
to church would find their doubts resolved; and there
was yarrow, which kept your lover true, particularly if
you plucked it with the proper ceremony from a young
man's grave.

Dona Ina remembered a fascinating volume of her
mother's time, the *Album Mexicana,* in which the senti-
mental properties of all flowers were set forth. "There
was the camelia, a beautiful woman without virtue, and
the pomegranate—"

"But the flowers of New Spain, Dona Ina, was there
nothing of these?" I insisted.

"Of a truth, yes, there was the cactus flower, not the
opunta, the broad-leaved spiny sort, of which hedges
were built in the old days, but the low, flamy-blos-
somed, prickly variety of hot sandy places. If a young
man wore such a one pinned upon his velvet jacket it
signified, 'I burn for you.'"

"And if he wore no flower at all, how then?"

Dona Ina laughed, "*Si me quieros, no me quieros*"; she referred to the common yellow composite which goes by the name of "sunshine," or in the San Joaquin, where miles of it mixed with blue phacelias brighten with the spring, as "flyflower." "In the old Spanish playing-cards," said Dona Ina, "the Jack of spades had such a one in his hand, but when I was a girl no caballero would have been caught saying, 'Love me, love me not!' They left all that to the señoritas."

There was a Castilian rose growing beside me. Now a Castilian rose is not in the least what you expect it to be. It is a thick, cabbagy florescence, the petals short and not recurved, the pink hardly deeper than that of the common wild rose, the leafage uninteresting. One has to remember that it distinguished itself long before the time of the tea and garden hybrids, and, I suspect, borrowed half its charm from the faces it set off. For there was never but one way in the world for a rose to be worn, and that is the way Castilian beauties discovered so long ago that centuries have not made any improvement in it. Set just behind the ear and discreetly veiled by the mantilla, it suggests the effulgent charm of Spain, tempered by mystery. The Señora Echivarra had followed my glance, and nodded acquiescence to my thought. "In dressing for a *baile,* one would have as soon left off the rose as one's fan. One wore it even when the dress was wreathed with other flowers."

"And did you, then, go wreathed in flowers?"

"Assuredly; from the garden if we had them, or from

the field. I remember once I was all blue larkspurs, here and here . . . " she illustrated on her person, "and long flat festoons of the *yerba buena* holding them together."

"It would have taken hoop skirts for that?" I opined.

"That also. It was the time that the waltz had been learned from the officers of the American ships, and we were quite wild about it. The good Padre had threatened to excommunicate us all if we danced it . . . but we danced . . . we danced. . . . " Dona Ina's pretty feet twitched reminiscently. The conversation wandered a long time in the past before it came back to the patio lying so still, divided from the street by the high wall, the clouding fig, and the gnarly pear tree. Beyond the artichokes a low partition wall shut off the vegetable plot; strings of chili reddened against it. There was not a blade of grass in sight, only the flat, black adobe paths worn smooth by generations of treading, house and enclosing walls all of one earth.

"But if so much came into the garden from the field, Señora, did nothing ever go out?"

Ah, yes, yes — the land is gracious; there was mustard of course, and pepper grass and horehound, blessed herb, which spread all over the west with healing. The pimpernel, too, crept out of the enclosing wall, and the tree mallow which came from the Channel Islands by way of the gardens and has become a common hedge plant on the sandy lands about the bay of San Francisco. Along streams which ran down from the unfenced gardens of the *Americanos,* callas had domesticated themselves and lifted their pure white spathes serenely amid a tangle of mint and wild blackberries and painted cup. The almond, the rude stock on which the tender sorts were grafted, if allowed to bear its worthless bitter nuts would take to hillsides naturally. It is not, after all, walls which hold gardens but water. This is all that constrains the commingling of wild and cultivated species; they care little for man, their benefactor. Give them water, said Dona Ina, and they come to your door like a fed dog, or if you like the figure better, like grateful children. They repay you with sweetness and healing.

A swift darted among the fig, marigolds, and portulacca of the inevitable rock-work which was the pride of the old Spanish gardens. Great rockets of tritoma flamed against the wall, on the other side of which traffic went unnoted and unsuspecting.

"But we, Dona Ina, we Americans, when we make a garden, make it in the sight of all so that all may have pleasure in it."

"Eh, the *Americanos* . . . " she shrugged; she moved to give a drink to the spotted musk, flowering in a chipped saucer; the subject did not interest her; her thought, like her flowers, had grown up in an enclosure.

{ ROSE 'BARON GIROD DE L'AIN' }

HOWARD NEMEROV

The Salt Garden

for S. M. S.

I

A good house, and ground whereon
With an amateur's toil
Both lawn and garden have been won
From a difficult, shallow soil
That, now inland, was once the shore
And once, maybe, the ocean floor.
Much patience, and some sweat,
Have made the garden green,
An even green the lawn.
Turnip and bean and violet
In a decent order set,
Grow, flourish and are gone;
Even the ruins of stalk and shell,
The vine when it goes brown,
Look civil and die well.
Sometimes in the late afternoon
I sit out with my wife,
Watching the work that we have done
Bend in the salt wind,
And think that here our life
Might be a long and happy one;
Though restless over the sand

The ocean's wrinkled green
Maneuvers in its sleep,
And I despise what I had planned,
Every work of the hand,
For what can man keep?

II

Restless, rising at dawn,
I saw the great gull come from the mist
To stand upon the lawn.
And there he shook his savage wing
To quiet, and stood like a high priest
Bird-masked, mantled in grey.
Before his fierce austerity
My thought bowed down, imagining
The wild sea lanes he wandered by
And the wild waters where he slept
Still as a candle in the crypt.
Noble, and not courteous,
He stared upon my green concerns,
Then, like a merchant prince
Come to some poor province,
Who, looking all about, discerns
No spice, no treasure house,
Nothing that can be made
Delightful to his haughty trade,
And so spreads out his sail,
Leaving to savage men
Their miserable regimen;

So did he rise, making a gale
About him by his wings,
And fought his huge freight into air
And vanished seaward with a cry—
A strange tongue but the tone clear.
He faded from my troubled eye
There where the ghostly sun
Came from the mist.
                    When he was gone
I turned back to the house
And thought of wife, of child,
And of my garden and my lawn
Serene in the wet dawn;
And thought that image of the wild
Wave where it beats the air
Had come, brutal, mysterious,
To teach the tenant gardener,
Green fellow of this paradise,
Where his salt dream lies.

Ripe Figs

Maman-Nainaine said that when the figs were ripe Babette might go to visit her cousins down on the Bayou-Lafourche where the sugar cane grows. Not that the ripening of figs had the least thing to do with it, but that is the way Maman-Nainaine was.

It seemed to Babette a very long time to wait; for the leaves upon the trees were tender yet, and the figs were like little hard, green marbles.

But warm rains came along and plenty of strong sunshine, and though Maman-Nainaine was as patient as the statue of la Madone, and Babette as restless as a humming-bird, the first thing they both knew it was hot summer-time. Every day Babette danced out to where the fig-trees were in a long line against the fence. She walked slowly beneath them, carefully peering between the gnarled, spreading branches. But each time she came disconsolate away again. What she saw there finally was something that made her sing and dance the whole long day.

When Maman-Nainaine sat down in her stately way to breakfast, the following morning, her muslin cap standing like an aureole about her white, placid face, Babette approached. She bore a dainty porcelain platter, which she set down before her godmother. It contained a dozen purple figs, fringed around with their rich, green leaves.

"Ah," said Maman-Nainaine arching her eyebrows, "how early the figs have ripened this year!"

"Oh," said Babette. "I think they have ripened very late."

"Babette," continued Maman-Nainaine, as she peeled the very plumpest figs with her pointed silver fruit-knife, "you will carry my love to them all down on Bayou-Lafourche. And tell your Tante Frosine I shall look for her at Toussaint—when the chrysanthemums are in bloom."

{ RED ABYSSINIAN BANANA }

O. HENRY

The Last Leaf

In a little district west of Washington Square the streets have run crazy and broken themselves into small strips called "places." These "places" make strange angles and curves. One street crosses itself a time or two. An artist once discovered a valuable possibility in this street. Suppose a collector with a bill for paints, paper, and canvas should, in traversing this route, suddenly meet himself coming back, without a cent having been paid on account!

So, to quaint old Greenwich Village the art people soon came prowling, hunting for north windows and eighteenth-century gables and Dutch attics and low rents. Then they imported some pewter mugs and a chafing dish or two from Sixth Avenue, and became a "colony."

At the top of a squatty, three-story brick Sue and Johnsy had their studio. "Johnsy" was familiar for

Joanna. One was from Maine; the other from California. They had met at the *table d'hôte* of an Eighth Street "Delmonico's," and found their tastes in art, chicory salad, and bishop sleeves so congenial that the joint studio resulted.

That was in May. In November a cold, unseen stranger, whom the doctors called Pneumonia, stalked about the colony, touching one here and there with his icy fingers. Over on the east side this ravager strode boldly, smiting his victims by scores, but his feet trod slowly through the maze of the narrow and moss-grown "places."

Mr. Pneumonia was not what you would call a chivalric old gentleman. A mite of a little woman with blood thinned by California zephyrs was hardly fair game for the red-fisted, short-breathed old duffer. But Johnsy he smote; and she lay, scarcely moving, on her painted iron bedstead, looking through the small Dutch window-panes at the blank side of the next brick house.

One morning the busy doctor invited Sue into the hallway with a shaggy, gray eyebrow.

"She has one chance in—let us say, ten," he said, as he shook down the mercury in his clinical thermometer. "And that chance is for her to want to live. This way people have of lining-up on the side of the undertaker makes the entire pharmacopœia look silly. Your little lady has made up her mind that she's not going to get well. Has she anything on her mind?"

"She—she wanted to paint the Bay of Naples some day," said Sue.

"Paint?—bosh! Has she anything on her mind worth thinking about twice—a man for instance?"

"A man?" said Sue, with a jew's-harp twang in her voice. "Is a man worth—but, no, doctor; there is nothing of the kind."

"Well, it is the weakness, then," said the doctor. "I will do all that science, so far as it may filter through my efforts, can accomplish. But whenever my patient begins to count the carriages in her funeral procession I subtract 50 percent from the curative power of medicines. If you will get her to ask one question about the new winter styles in cloak sleeves I will promise you a one-in-five chance for her, instead of one in ten."

After the doctor had gone Sue went into the workroom and cried a Japanese napkin to a pulp. Then she swaggered into Johnsy's room with her drawing board, whistling ragtime.

Johnsy lay, scarcely making a ripple under the bedclothes, with her face toward the window. Sue stopped whistling, thinking she was asleep.

She arranged her board and began a pen-and-ink drawing to illustrate a magazine story. Young artists must pave their way to Art by drawing pictures for magazine stories that young authors write to pave their way to Literature.

As Sue was sketching a pair of elegant horseshow riding trousers and a monocle on the figure of the hero, an Idaho cowboy, she heard a low sound, several times repeated. She went quickly to the bedside.

Johnsy's eyes were open wide. She was looking out the window and counting—counting backward.

"Twelve," she said, and a little later "eleven"; and then "ten," and "nine"; and then "eight" and "seven," almost together.

Sue looked solicitously out of the window. What was there to count? There was only a bare, dreary yard to be seen, and the blank side of the brick house twenty feet away. An old, old ivy vine, gnarled and decayed at the roots, climbed half way up the brick wall. The cold breath of autumn had stricken its leaves from the vine until its skeleton branches clung, almost bare, to the crumbling bricks.

"What is it, dear?" asked Sue.

"Six," said Johnsy, in almost a whisper. "They're falling faster now. Three days ago there were almost a hundred. It made my head ache to count them. But now it's easy. There goes another one. There are only five left now."

"Five what, dear? Tell your Sudie."

"Leaves. On the ivy vine. When the last one falls I must go, too. I've known that for three days. Didn't the doctor tell you?"

"Oh, I never heard of such nonsense," complained Sue, with magnificent scorn. "What have old ivy leaves to do with your getting well? And you used to love that vine so, you naughty girl. Don't be a goosey. Why, the doctor told me this morning that your chances for getting well real soon were—let's see exactly what he said—he said the chances were ten to one! Why, that's almost as good a chance as we have in New York when we ride on the street cars or walk past a new building. Try to take some broth now, and let Sudie go back to her drawing, so she can sell the editor man with it, and buy port wine for her sick child, and pork chops for her greedy self."

"You needn't get any more wine," said Johnsy, keeping her eyes fixed out the window. "There goes another. No, I don't want any broth. That leaves just four. I want to see the last one fall before it gets dark. Then I'll go, too."

"Johnsy, dear," said Sue, bending over her, "will you promise me to keep your eyes closed, and not look out the window until I am done working? I must hand those drawings in by to-morrow. I need the light, or I would draw the shade down."

"Couldn't you draw in the other room?" asked Johnsy, coldly.

"I'd rather be here by you," said Sue. "Besides, I don't want you to keep looking at those silly ivy leaves."

"Tell me as soon as you have finished," said Johnsy, closing her eyes, and lying white and still as a fallen statue, "because I want to see the last one fall. I'm tired of waiting. I'm tired of thinking. I want to turn loose my hold on everything, and go sailing down, down, just like one of those poor, tired leaves."

"Try to sleep," said Sue. "I must call Behrman up to be my model for the old hermit miner. I'll not be gone a minute. Don't try to move 'til I come back."

Old Behrman was a painter who lived on the ground floor beneath them. He was past sixty and had a Michael Angelo's Moses beard curling down from the head of a satyr along the body of an imp. Behrman was a failure in art. Forty years he had wielded the brush without getting near enough to touch the hem of his Mistress's robe. He had been always about to paint a masterpiece, but had never yet begun it. For several years he had painted nothing except now and then a daub in the line of commerce or advertising. He earned a little by serving as a model to those young artists in the colony who could not pay the price of a professional. He drank gin to excess, and still talked of his coming masterpiece. For the rest he was a fierce little old man, who scoffed terribly at softness in any one, and who regarded himself as especial mastiff-in-waiting to protect the two young artists in the studio above.

Sue found Behrman smelling strongly of juniper berries in his dimly lighted den below. In one corner was a blank canvas on an easel that had been waiting there for twenty-five years to receive the first line of the masterpiece. She told him of Johnsy's fancy, and how she feared she would, indeed, light and fragile as a leaf herself, float away, when her slight hold upon the world grew weaker.

Old Behrman, with his red eyes plainly streaming, shouted his contempt and derision for such idiotic imaginings.

"Vass!" he cried. "Is dere people in de world mit der foolishness to die because leafs dey drop off from a confounded vine? I haf not heard of such a thing. No, I will not bose as a model for your fool hermit-dunderhead. Vy do you allow dot silly pusiness to come in der brain of her? Ach, dot poor leetle Miss Yohnsy."

"She is very ill and weak," said Sue, "and the fever has left her mind morbid and full of strange fancies.

Very well, Mr. Behrman, if you do not care to pose for me, you needn't. But I think you are a horrid old—old flibbertigibbet."

"You are just like a woman!" yelled Behrman. "Who said I will not bose? Go on. I come mit you. For half an hour I haf peen trying to say dot I am ready to bose. Gott! dis is not any blace in which one so goot as Miss Yohnsy shall lie sick. Some day I vill baint a master-piece, and ve shall all go away. Gott! yes."

Johnsy was sleeping when they went upstairs. Sue pulled the shade down to the window-sill, and motioned Behrman into the other room. In there they peered out the window fearfully at the ivy vine. Then they looked at each other for a moment without speaking. A persistent, cold rain was falling, mingled with snow. Behrman, in his old blue shirt, took his seat as the hermit miner on an upturned kettle for a rock.

When Sue awoke from an hour's sleep the next morning she found Johnsy with dull, wide-open eyes staring at the drawn green shade.

"Pull it up; I want to see," she ordered, in a whisper.

Wearily Sue obeyed.

But, lo! after the beating rain and fierce gusts of wind that had endured through the livelong night, there yet stood out against the brick wall one ivy leaf. It was the last on the vine. Still dark green near its stem, but with its serrated edges tinted with the yellow of dissolu-tion and decay, it hung bravely from a branch some twenty feet above the ground.

"It is the last one," said Johnsy. "I thought it would

surely fall during the night. I heard the wind. It will fall to-day, and I shall die at the same time."

"Dear, dear!" said Sue, leaning her worn face down to the pillow, "think of me, if you won't think of yourself. What would I do?"

But Johnsy did not answer. The lonesomest thing in all the world is a soul when it is making ready to go on its mysterious, far journey. The fancy seemed to possess her more strongly as one by one the ties that bound her to friendship and to earth were loosed.

The day wore away, and even through the twilight they could see the lone ivy leaf clinging to its stem against the wall. And then, with the coming of the night the north wind was again loosed, while the rain still beat against the windows and pattered down from the low Dutch eaves.

When it was light enough Johnsy, the merciless, commanded that the shade be raised.

The ivy leaf was still there.

Johnsy lay for a long time looking at it. And then she called to Sue, who was stirring her chicken broth over the gas stove.

"I've been a bad girl, Sudie," said Johnsy. "Something has made that last leaf stay there to show me how wicked I was. It is a sin to want to die. You may bring me a little broth now, and some milk with a little port in it, and—no; bring me a hand-mirror first, and then pack some pillows about me, and I will sit up and watch you cook."

An hour later she said:

"Sudie, some day I hope to paint the Bay of Naples."

The doctor came in the afternoon, and Sue had an excuse to go into the hallway as he left.

"Even chances," said the doctor, taking Sue's thin, shaking hand in his. "With good nursing you'll win. And now I must see another case I have downstairs. Behrman, his name is—some kind of an artist, I believe. Pneumonia, too. He is an old, weak man, and the attack is acute. There is no hope for him; but he goes to the hospital to-day to be made more comfortable."

The next day the doctor said to Sue: "She's out of danger. You've won. Nutrition and care now—that's all."

And that afternoon Sue came to the bed where Johnsy lay, contentedly knitting a very blue and very useless woollen shoulder scarf, and put one arm around her, pillows and all.

"I have something to tell you, white mouse," she said. "Mr. Behrman died of pneumonia to-day in the hospital. He was ill only two days. The janitor found him on the morning of the first day in his room downstairs helpless with pain. His shoes and clothing were wet through and icy cold. They couldn't imagine where he had been on such a dreadful night. And then they found a lantern, still lighted, and a ladder that had been dragged from its place, and some scattered brushes, and a palette with green and yellow colors mixed on it, and—look out the window, dear, at the last ivy leaf on the wall. Didn't you wonder why it never fluttered or moved when the wind blew? Ah, darling, it's Behrman's masterpiece—he painted it there the night that the last leaf fell."

AMY CLAMPITT

The Horned Rampion

Daily, out of that unfamiliar,
entrancingly perpendicular
terrain, some new
and, on minute
inspection, marvelous
thing would be opening—

yet another savory-
flowery permutation
of selene or salvia,
of scabious, of rockrose,
of evening primrose, of
bellflower such as the one

I'd never before laid eyes
on the like of: spurred,
spirily airy, a sort of
stemborne baldachin,
a lone, poised,
hovering rarity, hued

midway between the clear
azure of the rosemary
and the aquilegia's
somberer purple,
that turned out to be
named the horned rampion.

Next day it was no longer
singular but several;
the day after, many.
Within a week it was
everywhere, had become
the mere horned rampion,

had grown so familiar
I forgot it, had not
thought of it since,
it seems, until the moment
a volume of the Encyclopedia
Britannica, pulled down

for some purpose, fell open
at random, and there was
the horned rampion, named
and depicted, astonishing
in memory as old love
reopened, still quivering.

{ IRIS 'MARTILE ROWLAND' }

EUGENIA COLLIER

Marigolds

When I think of the hometown of my youth, all that I seem to remember is dust—the brown, crumbly dust of late summer—arid, sterile dust that gets into the eyes and makes them water, gets into the throat and between the toes of bare brown feet. I don't know why I should remember only the dust. Surely there must have been lush green lawns and paved streets under leafy shade trees somewhere in town; but memory is an abstract painting—it does not present things as they are, but rather as they *feel*. And so, when I think of that time and that place, I remember only the dry September of the dirt roads and grassless yards of the shantytown where I lived. And one other thing I remember, another incongruency of memory—a brilliant splash of sunny yellow against the dust—Miss Lottie's marigolds.

Whenever the memory of those marigolds flashes across my mind, a strange nostalgia comes with it and remains long after the picture has faded. I feel again the chaotic emotions of adolescence, illusive as smoke, yet as real as the potted geranium before me now. Joy and rage and wild animal gladness and shame become tangled together in the multicolored skein of fourteen-going-on-fifteen as I recall that devastating moment when I was suddenly more woman than child, years ago in Miss Lottie's yard. I think of those marigolds at the strangest times; I remember them vividly now as I desperately pass away the time waiting for you, who will not come.

I suppose that futile waiting was the sorrowful background music of our impoverished little community when I was young. The Depression that gripped the nation was no new thing to us, for the black workers of rural Maryland had always been depressed. I don't know what it was that we were waiting for; certainly not for the prosperity that was "just around the corner," for those were white folks' words, which we never believed. Nor did we wait for hard work and thrift to pay off in shining success as the American Dream promised, for we knew better than that, too. Perhaps we waited for a miracle, amorphous in concept but necessary if one was to have the grit to rise before dawn each day and labor in the white man's vineyard until after dark, or to wander about in the September dust offering one's sweat in return for some meager share of bread. But God was chary with miracles in those days, and so we waited—and waited.

We children, of course, were only vaguely aware of the extent of our poverty. Having no radios, few newspapers, and no magazines, we were somewhat unaware of the world outside our community. Nowadays we would be called "culturally deprived" and people would write books and hold conferences about us. In those days everybody we knew was just as hungry and ill clad as we were. Poverty was the cage in which we all were trapped, and our hatred of it was still the vague, undirected restlessness of the zoo-bred flamingo who knows that nature created him to fly free.

As I think of those days I feel most poignantly the tag-end of summer, the bright dry times when we began to have a sense of shortening days and the imminence of the cold.

By the time I was fourteen my brother Joey and I were the only children left at our house, the older ones having left home for early marriage or the lure of the city, and the two babies having been sent to relatives who might care for them better than we. Joey was three years younger than I, and a boy, and therefore vastly inferior. Each morning our mother and father trudged wearily down the dirt road and around the bend, she to her domestic job, he to his daily unsuccessful quest for work. After our few chores around the tumbledown shanty, Joey and I were free to run wild in the sun with other children similarly situated.

For the most part, those days are ill defined in my memory, running together and combining like a fresh watercolor painting left out in the rain. I remember squatting in the road drawing a picture in the dust, a picture which Joey gleefully erased with one sweep of his dirty foot. I remember fishing for minnows in a muddy creek and watching madly as they eluded my cupped hands, while Joey laughed uproariously. And I remember, that year, a strange restlessness of body and of spirit, a feeling that something old and familiar was ending, and something unknown and therefore terrifying was beginning.

One day returns to me with special clarity for some reason, perhaps because it was the beginning of the experience that in some inexplicable way marked the end of innocence. I was loafing under the great oak tree in our yard, deep in some reverie which I have now forgotten, except that it involved some secret, secret thoughts of one of the Harris boys across the yard. Joey and a bunch of kids were bored now with the old tire suspended from an oak limb which had kept them entertained for a while.

"Hey, Lizabeth," Joey yelled. He never talked when he could yell. "Hey, Lizabeth, let's go somewhere."

I came reluctantly from my private world. "Where you want to go? What you want to do?"

The truth was that we were becoming tired of the formlessness of our summer days. The idleness whose prospect had seemed so beautiful during the busy days of spring now had degenerated to an almost desperate effort to fill up the empty midday hours.

"Let's go see can we find some locusts on the hill," someone suggested.

Joey was scornful. "Ain't no more locusts there. Y'all got 'em all while they was still green."

The argument that followed was brief and not really worth the effort. Hunting locust trees wasn't fun anymore by now.

"Tell you what," said Joey finally, his eyes sparkling. "Let's us go over to Miss Lottie's."

The idea caught on at once, for annoying Miss Lottie was always fun. I was still child enough to scamper along with the group over rickety fences and through bushes that tore our already raggedy clothes, back to where Miss Lottie lived. I think now that we must have made a tragicomic spectacle, five or six kids of different ages, each of us clad in only one garment— the girls in faded dresses that were too long or too short, the boys in patchy pants, their sweaty brown chests gleaming in the hot sun. A little cloud of dust followed our thin legs and bare feet as we tramped over the barren land.

When Miss Lottie's house came into view we stopped, ostensibly to plan our strategy, but actually to reinforce our courage. Miss Lottie's house was the most ramshackle of all our ramshackle homes. The sun and rain had long since faded its rickety frame siding from white to a sullen gray. The boards themselves seemed to remain upright, not from being nailed together, but rather from leaning together like a house that a child might have constructed from cards. A brisk wind might have blown it down, and the fact that it was still standing implied a kind of enchantment that was stronger than the elements. There it stood, and far as I know is standing yet—a gray rotting thing with no porch, no shutters, no steps, set on a cramped lot with no grass, not even any weeds — a monument to decay.

In front of the house in a squeaky rocking chair sat Miss Lottie's son, John Burke, completing the impression of decay. John Burke was what was known as "queer-headed." Black and ageless, he sat, rocking day in and day out in a mindless stupor, lulled by the monotonous squeak-squawk of the chair. A battered hat atop his shaggy head shaded him from the sun. Usually John Burke was totally unaware of everything outside his quiet dream world. But if you disturbed him, if you intruded upon his fantasies, he would become enraged, strike out at you, and curse at you in some strange enchanted language which only he could understand. We children made a game of thinking of ways to disturb John Burke and then to elude his violent retribution.

But our real fun and our real fear lay in Miss Lottie herself. Miss Lottie seemed to be at least a hundred years old. Her big frame still held traces of the tall, powerful woman she must have been in youth, although it was now bent and drawn. Her smooth skin was a dark reddish-brown, and her face had Indian-like features and the stern stoicism that one associates with Indian faces. Miss Lottie didn't like intruders either, especially children. She never left her yard, and nobody ever visited her. We never knew how she managed those necessities which depend on human interaction — how she ate, for example, or even whether she ate. When we were tiny children, we thought Miss Lottie was a witch and we made up tales, that we half believed ourselves, about her exploits. We were far too sophisticated now, of course, to believe the witch-nonsense. But old fears have a way of clinging like cobwebs, and so when we sighted the tumbledown shack, we had to stop to reinforce our nerves.

"Look, there she is," I whispered, forgetting that Miss Lottie could not possibly have heard me from that distance. "She's fooling with them crazy flowers."

"Yeh, look at 'er."

Miss Lottie's marigolds were perhaps the strangest part of the picture. Certainly they did not fit in with the crumbling decay of the rest of her yard. Beyond the dusty brown yard, in front of the sorry gray house, rose suddenly and shockingly a dazzling strip of bright blossoms, clumped together in enormous mounds, warm and passionate and sun-golden. The old black witch-woman worked on them all summer, every summer, down on her creaky knees, weeding and cultivating and arranging, while the house crumbled and John Burke rocked. For some perverse reason, we children hated those marigolds. They interfered with the perfect ugliness of the place; they were too beautiful; they said too much that we could not understand; they did not make sense. There was something in the vigor with which the old woman destroyed the weeds that intimidated us. It should have been a comical sight—the old woman with the man's hat on her cropped white head, leaning over the bright mounds, her big backside in the air—but it wasn't comical, it was something we could not name. We had to annoy her by whizzing a pebble into her flowers or by yelling a dirty word, then dancing away from her rage, reveling in our youth and mocking her age. Actually, I think it was the flowers we wanted to destroy, but nobody had the nerve to try it, not even Joey, who was usually fool enough to try anything.

"Y'all git some stones," commanded Joey now, and was met with instant giggling obedience as everyone except me began to gather pebbles from the dusty ground. "Come on, Lizabeth."

I just stood there peering through the bushes, torn between wanting to join the fun and feeling that it was all a bit silly.

"You scared, Lizabeth?"

I cursed and spat on the ground—my favorite gesture of phony bravado. "Y'all children get the stones, I'll show you how to use 'em."

I said before that we children were not consciously aware of how thick were the bars of our cage. I wonder now, though, whether we were not more aware of it than I thought. Perhaps we had some dim notion of what we were, and how little chance we had of being anything else. Otherwise, why would we have been so preoccupied with destruction? Anyway, the pebbles were collected quickly, and everybody looked at me to begin the fun.

"Come on, y'all."

We crept to the edge of the bushes that bordered the narrow road in front of Miss Lottie's place. She was working placidly, kneeling over the flowers, her dark hand plunged into the golden mound. Suddenly—

zing — an expertly aimed stone cut the head off one of the blossoms.

"Who out there?" Miss Lottie's backside came down and her head came up as her sharp eyes searched the bushes. "You better git!"

We had crouched down out of sight in the bushes, where we stifled the giggles that insisted on coming. Miss Lottie gazed warily across the road for a moment, then cautiously returned to her weeding. *Zing* — Joey sent a pebble into the blooms, and another marigold was beheaded.

Miss Lottie was enraged now. She began struggling to her feet, leaning on a rickety cane and shouting, "Y'all git! Go on home!" Then the rest of the kids let loose with their pebbles, storming the flowers and laughing wildly and senselessly at Miss Lottie's impotent rage. She shook her stick at us and started shakily toward the road crying, "Git 'long! John Burke! John Burke, come help!"

Then I lost my head entirely, mad with the power of inciting such rage, and ran out of the bushes in the storm of pebbles, straight towards Miss Lottie, chanting madly, "Old witch, fell in a ditch, picked up a penny and thought she was rich!" The children screamed with delight, dropped their pebbles, and joined the crazy dance, swarming around Miss Lottie like bees and chanting, "Old lady witch!" while she screamed curses at us. The madness lasted only a moment, for John Burke, startled at last, lurched out of his chair, and we dashed for the bushes just as Miss Lottie's cane went whizzing at my head.

I did not join the merriment when the kids gathered again under the oak in our bare yard. Suddenly I was ashamed, and I did not like being ashamed. The child in me sulked and said it was all in fun, but the woman in me flinched at the thought of the malicious attack that I had led. The mood lasted all afternoon. When we ate the beans and rice that was supper that night, I did not notice my father's silence, for he was always silent these days, nor did I notice my mother's absence, for she always worked until well into evening. Joey and I had a particularly bitter argument after supper; his exuberance got on my nerves. Finally I stretched out on the pallet in the room we shared and fell into a fitful doze.

When I awoke, somewhere in the middle of the night, my mother had returned, and I vaguely listened to the conversation that was audible through the thin walls that separated our rooms. At first I heard no words, only voices. My mother's voice was like a cool, dark room in summer—peaceful, soothing, quiet. I loved to listen to it; it made things seem all right somehow. But my father's voice cut through hers, shattering the peace.

"Twenty-two years, Maybelle, twenty-two years," he was saying, "and I got nothing for you, nothing, nothing."

"It's all right, honey, you'll get something. Everybody out of work now, you know that."

"It ain't right. Ain't no man ought to eat his woman's food year in and year out, and see his children running wild. Ain't nothing right about that."

"Honey, you took good care of us when you had it. Ain't nobody got nothing nowadays."

"I ain't talking about nobody else, I'm talking about *me*. God knows I try." My mother said something I could not hear, and my father cried out louder, "What must a man do, tell me that?"

"Look, we ain't starving. I git paid every week, and Mrs. Ellis is real nice about giving me things. She gonna let me have Mr. Ellis's old coat for you this winter—"

"Damn Mr. Ellis's coat! And damn his money! You think I want white folks' leavings? Damn, Maybelle"— and suddenly he sobbed, loudly and painfully, and cried helplessly and hopelessly in the dark night. I had never heard a man cry before. I did not know men ever cried. I covered my ears with my hands but could not cut off the sound of my father's harsh, painful, despairing sobs. My father was a strong man who could whisk a child upon his shoulders and go singing through the house. My father whittled toys for us and laughed so loud that the great oak seemed to laugh with him, and taught us how to fish and hunt rabbits. How could it be that my father was crying? But the sobs went on, unstifled, finally quieting until I could hear my mother's voice, deep and rich, humming softly as she used to hum for a frightened child.

The world had lost its boundary lines. My mother, who was small and soft, was now the strength of the family; my father, who was the rock on which the family had been built, was sobbing like the tiniest child. Everything was suddenly out of tune, like a broken accordion. Where did I fit into this crazy picture? I do

107

not now remember my thoughts, only a feeling of great bewilderment and fear.

Long after the sobbing and the humming had stopped, I lay on the pallet, still as stone, with my hands over my ears, wishing that I too could cry and be comforted. The night was silent now except for the sound of the crickets and of Joey's soft breathing. But the room was too crowded with fear to allow me to sleep, and finally, feeling the terrible aloneness of 4 a.m., I decided to awaken Joey.

"Ouch! What's the matter with you? What you want?" he demanded disagreeably when I had pinched and slapped him awake.

"Come on, wake up."

"What for? Go 'way."

I was lost for a reasonable reply. I could not say, "I'm scared and I don't want to be alone," so I merely said, "I'm going out. If you want to come, come on."

The promise of adventure awoke him. "Going out now? Where to, Lizabeth? What you going to do?"

I was pulling my dress over my head. Until now I had not thought of going out. "Just come on," I replied tersely.

I was out the window and halfway down the road before Joey caught up with me.

"Wait, Lizabeth, where you going?"

I was running as if the Furies were after me, as perhaps they were—running silently and furiously until I came to where I had half-known I was headed: to Miss Lottie's yard.

The half-dawn light was more eerie than complete darkness, and in it the old house was like the ruin that my world had become—foul and crumbling, a grotesque caricature. It looked haunted, but I was not afraid, because I was haunted, too.

"Lizabeth, you lost your mind?" panted Joey.

I had indeed lost my mind, for all the smoldering emotions of that summer swelled in me and burst—the great need for my mother, who was never there; the hopelessness of our poverty and degradation; the bewilderment of being neither child nor woman and yet both at once; the fear unleashed by my father's tears. And these feelings combined in one great impulse toward destruction.

"Lizabeth!"

I leaped furiously into the mounds of marigolds and pulled madly, trampling and pulling and destroying the perfect yellow blooms. The fresh smell of early morning and of dew-soaked marigolds spurred me on as I went tearing and mangling and sobbing while Joey tugged my dress or my waist crying, "Lizabeth, stop, please stop!"

And then I was sitting in the ruined little garden among the uprooted and ruined flowers, crying and crying, and it was too late to undo what I had done. Joey was sitting beside me, silent and frightened, not knowing what to say. Then: "Lizabeth, look."

I opened my swollen eyes and saw in front of me a pair of large calloused feet; my gaze lifted to the swollen legs, the age-distorted body clad in a tight cotton nightdress, and then the shadowed Indian face surrounded by stubby white hair. There was no rage in the face now, now that the garden was destroyed and there was nothing any longer to be protected.

"M-miss Lottie!" I scrambled to my feet and just stood there and stared at her, and that was the moment when childhood faded and womanhood began. That violent, crazy act was the last act of childhood. For as I gazed at the immobile face with the sad, weary eyes, I gazed upon a kind of reality which is hidden to childhood. The witch was no longer a witch but only a broken old woman who had dared to create beauty in the midst of ugliness and sterility. She had been born in squalor and lived in it all her life. Now at the end of that life she had nothing except a falling-down hut, a wrecked body, and John Burke, the mindless son of her passion. Whatever verve there was left in her, whatever was of love and beauty and joy that had not been squeezed out by life had been there in the marigolds she had so tenderly cared for.

Of course I could not express the thing that I knew about Miss Lottie as I stood there awkward and ashamed. The years have put words to the things I knew in that moment, and as I look back upon it, I know that that moment marked the end of innocence. People think of the loss of innocence as meaning the loss of virginity, but this is far from true. Innocence involves an unseeing acceptance of things at face value, an ignorance of the area below the surface. In that humiliating moment I looked beyond myself and into the depths of another person. This was the beginning of compassion, and one cannot have both compassion and innocence.

The years have taken me worlds away from that time and that place, from the dust and squalor of our lives and from the bright thing that I destroyed in a blind childish striking out at God-knows-what. Miss Lottie died long ago and many years have passed since I last saw her hut, completely barren at last, for despite my wild contrition she never planted marigolds again. Yet there are times when the image of those passionate yellow mounds returns with a painful poignancy. For one does not have to be ignorant and poor to find that this life is barren as the dusty yards of our town. And I too have planted marigolds.

SYLVIA PLATH

Fable of the Rhododendron Stealers

I walked the unwalked garden of rose-beds
In the public park; at home felt the want
Of a single rose present to imagine
The garden's remainder in full paint.

The stone lion-head set in the wall
Let drop its spittle of sluggish green
Into the stone basin. I snipped
An orange bud, pocketed it. When

It had opened its orange in my vase,
Retrogressed to blowze, I next chose red;
Argued my conscience clear which robbed
The park of less red than withering did.

Musk satisfied my nose, red my eye,
The petals' nap my fingertips:
I considered the poetry I rescued
From blind air, from complete eclipse.

Yet today, a yellow bud in my hand,
I stalled at sudden noisy crashes
From the laurel thicket. No one approached.
A spasm took the rhododendron bushes:

Three girls, engrossed, were wrenching full clusters
Of cerise and pink from the rhododendron,
Mountaining them on spread newspaper.
They brassily picked, slowed by no chagrin,

And wouldn't pause for my straight look.
But gave me pause, my rose a charge,
Whether nicety stood confounded by love,
Or petty thievery by large.

{ COLOCASIA 'BLACK MAGIC' }

ROBERT GRAVES

Earth to Earth

Yes, yes and yes! Don't get me wrong, for goodness' sake. I am heart and soul with you. I agree that Man is wickedly defrauding the Earth-Mother of her ancient dues by not putting back into the soil as much nourishment as he takes out. And that modern plumbing is, if you like, a running sore in the body politic. And that municipal incinerators are genocidal rather than germicidal. . . . And that cremation should be made a capital crime. And that dustbowls created by the greedy plough . . .

. . . Yes, yes and yes again. *But!*

Elsie and Roland Hedge—she a book-illustrator, he an architect with suspect lungs—had been warned against Dr. Eugen Steinpilz. "He'll bring you no luck," I told them. "My little finger says so decisively."

"You too?" asked Elsie indignantly. (This was at

Brixham, South Devon, in March 1940.) "I suppose you think that because of his foreign accent and his beard he must be a spy?"

"No," I said coldly, "that point hadn't occurred to me. But I won't contradict you."

The very next day Elsie deliberately picked a friendship—I don't like the phrase, but that's what she did—with the Doctor, an Alsatian with an American passport, who described himself as a *Naturphilosoph*; and both she and Ronald were soon immersed in Steinpilzerei up to the nostrils. It began when he invited them to lunch and gave them cold meat and two rival sets of vegetable dishes—potatoes (baked), carrots (creamed), bought from the local fruiterer; and potatoes (baked) and carrots (creamed), grown on compost in his own garden.

The superiority of the latter over the former in appearance, size, and especially flavour came as an eye-opener to Elsie and Roland. Yes, and yes, I know just how they felt. Why shouldn't I? When I visit the market here in Palma, I always refuse La Torre potatoes, because they are raised for the early English market and therefore reek of imported chemical fertilizer. Instead I buy Son Sardina potatoes, which taste as good as the ones we used to get in England fifty years ago. The reason is that the Son Sardina farmers manure their fields with Palma kitchen-refuse, still available by the cartload—this being too backward a city to afford effective modern methods of destroying it.

Thus Dr. Steinpilz converted the childless and devoted couple to the Steinpilz method of composting. It did not, as a matter of fact, vary greatly from the methods you read about in the *Gardening Notes* of your favourite national newspaper, except that it was far more violent. Dr. Steinpilz had invented a formula for producing extremely fierce bacteria, capable (Roland claimed) of breaking down an old boot or the family Bible or a torn woollen vest into beautiful black humus almost as you watched. The formula could not be bought, however, and might be communicated under oath of secrecy only to members of the Eugen Steinpilz Fellowship—which I refused to join. I won't pretend therefore to know the formula myself, but one night I overheard Elsie and Roland arguing across the hedge as to whether the planetary influences were favourable; and they also mentioned a ram's horn in which, it seems, a complicated mixture of triturated animal and vegetable products— technically called "the Mother"—was to be cooked up. I gather also that a bull's foot and a goat's pancreas were part of the works, because Mr. Pook the butcher afterwards told me that he had been puzzled by Roland's request for these unusual cuts. Milkwort and pennyroyal and bee-orchid and vetch certainly figured among the Mother's herbal ingredients; I recognized these one day in a gardening basket Elsie had left in the post office.

The Hedges soon had their first compost heap cooking away in the garden, which was about the size of a tennis-court and consisted mostly of well-kept lawn. Dr. Steinpilz, who supervised, now began to haunt the cottage like the smell of drains; I had to give up calling on them. Then, after the Fall of France, Brixham became a war-zone whence everyone but us British and our Free French or Free Belgian allies were extruded. Consequently Dr. Steinpilz had to leave; which he did with very bad grace, and was killed in a Liverpool air-raid the day before he should have sailed back to New York. But that was far from closing the ledger. I think Elsie must have been in love with the Doctor, and certainly Roland had a hero-worship for him. They treasured a signed collection of all his esoteric books, each called after a different semi-precious stone, and used to read them out aloud to each other at meals, in turns. Then to show that this was a practical philosophy, not just random assemblage of beautiful thoughts about Nature, they began composting in a deeper and even more religious way than before. The lawn had come up, of course; but they used the sods to sandwich layers of kitchen waste, which they mixed with the scrapings from an abandoned pigsty, two barrowfuls of sodden poplar leaves from the recreation ground, and a sack of rotten turnips. Looking over the hedge, I caught the fanatic gleam in Elsie's eye as she turned the hungry bacteria loose on the heap, and could not repress a premonitory shudder.

So far, not too bad, perhaps. But when serious bombing started and food became so scarce that house-wives were fined for not making over their swill to the national pigs, Elsie and Roland grew worried. Having already abandoned their ordinary sanitary system and built an earth-closet in the garden, they now tried to convince neighbours of their duty to do the same, even at the risk of catching cold and getting spiders down the

neck. Elsie also sent Roland after the slow-moving Red
Devon cows as they lurched home along the lane at
dusk, to rescue the precious droppings with a kitchen
shovel; while she visited the local ash-dump with a
packing case mounted on wheels, and collected whatever she found there of an organic nature—dead cats,
old rags, withered flowers, cabbage stalks, and such
household waste as even a national wartime pig would
have coughed at. She also saved every drop of their
bath-water for sprinkling the heaps; because it contained, she said, valuable animal salts.

The test of a good compost heap, as every illuminate
knows, is whether a certain revolting-looking, if benefi-
cial, fungus sprouts from it. Elsie's heaps were grey with
this crop, and so hot inside that they could be used for
haybox cookery; which must have saved her a deal of
fuel. I call them "Elsie's heaps" because she now considered herself Dr. Steinpilz's earthly delegate; and loyal
Roland did not dispute this claim.

A critical stage in the story came during the Blitz. It
will be remembered that trainloads of Londoners, who
had been evacuated to South Devon when war broke
out, thereafter de-evacuated and re-evacuated and re-
de-evacuated themselves, from time to time, in a most
disorganized fashion. Elsie and Roland, as it happened,
escaped having evacuees billeted on them, because they
had no spare bedroom; but one night an old naval pen-
sioner came knocking at their door and demanded lodg-
ing for the night. Having been burned out of Plymouth,
where everything was chaos, he had found himself

walking away and blundering along in a daze until he fetched up here, hungry and dead-beat. They gave him a meal and bedded him on the sofa; but when Elsie came down in the morning to fork over the heaps, she found him dead of heart-failure.

Roland broke a long silence by coming, in some embarrassment, to ask my advice. Elsie, he said, had decided that it would be wrong to trouble the police about the case; because the police were so busy these days, and the poor old fellow had claimed to possess neither kith nor kin. So they'd read the burial service over him and, after removing his belt-buckle, trouser buttons, metal spectacle-case, and a bunch of keys, which were irreducible, had laid him reverently in the new compost heap. Its other contents, he added, were a cartload of waste from the cider-factory, salvaged cow-dung, and several basketfuls of hedge clippings. Had they done wrong?

"If you mean 'will I report you the Civil Authorities?' the answer is no," I assured him. "I wasn't looking over the hedge at the relevant hour, and what you tell me is only hearsay." Roland shambled off satisfied.

The War went on. Not only did the Hedges convert the whole garden into serried rows of Eugen Steinpilz memorial heaps, leaving no room for planting the pota-toes or carrots to which the compost had been prospec-tively devoted, but they scavenged the offal from the Brixham fish-market and salvaged the contents of the bin outside the surgical ward at the Cottage Hospital. Every spring, I remember, Elsie used to pick big bunches of primroses and put them straight on the compost, without even a last wistful sniff; virgin primroses were supposed to be particularly relished by the fierce bacteria.

Here the story becomes a little painful for members, say, of a family reading circle; I will soften it as much as possible. One morning a policeman called on the Hedges with a summons, and I happened to see Roland peep anxiously out of the bedroom window, but quickly pull his head in again. The policeman rang and knocked and waited, then tried the back door; and presently went away. The summons was for a black-out offence, but apparently the Hedges did not know this. Next morning he called again, and when nobody answered, forced the lock of the back door. They were found dead in bed together, having taken an overdose of sleeping tablets. A note on the coverlet ran simply:

> Please lay our bodies on the heap nearest the pigsty. Flowers by request. Strew some on the bodies, mixed with a little kitchen waste, and then fork the earth lightly over.
>
> E.H.; R.H.

George Irks, the new tenant, proposed to grow potatoes and dig for victory. He hired a cart and began throwing the compost into the River Dart, "not liking the look of them toadstools," as he subsequently explained. The five beautifully clean human skeletons which George unearthed in the process were still awaiting identification when the War ended.

BILLY COLLINS

Bonsai

All it takes is one to throw a room
completely out of whack.

Over by the window
it looks hundreds of yards away,

a lone stark gesture of wood
on the distant cliff of a table.

Up close, it draws you in,
cuts everything down to its size.

Look at it from the doorway,
and the world dilates and bloats.

The button lying next to it
is now a pearl wheel,

the book of matches is a raft,
and the coffee cup a cistern

to catch the same rain
that moistens its small plot of dark, mossy earth.

For it even carries its own weather,
leaning away from a fierce wind

that somehow blows
through the calm tropics of this room.

The way it bends inland at the elbow
makes me want to inch my way

to the very top of its spiky greenery,
hold onto for dear life

and watch the sea storm rage,
hoping for a tiny whale to appear.

I want to see her plunging forward
through the troughs,

tunneling under the foam and spindrift
on her annual, thousand-mile journey.

{ TRILLIUM UNDERWOODII }

JOHN UPDIKE

Leaves

The grape leaves outside my window are curiously beautiful. "Curiously" because it comes upon me as strange, after the long darkness of self-absorption and fear and shame in which I have been living, that things are beautiful, that independent of our catastrophes they continue to maintain the casual precision, the effortless abundance of inventive "effect," which is the hallmark and specialty of Nature. Nature: this morning it seems to me very clear that Nature may be defined as that which exists without guilt. Our bodies are in Nature; our shoes, their laces, the little plastic tips of the laces—everything around us and about us is in Nature, and yet something holds us away from it, like the upward push of water which keeps us from touching the sandy bottom, ribbed and glimmering with crescental fragments of oyster shell, so clear to our eyes.

A blue jay lights on a twig outside my window.

Momentarily sturdy, he stands astraddle, his dingy rump toward me, his head alertly frozen in silhouette, the predatory curve of his beak stamped on a sky almost white above the misting tawny marsh. See him? I do, and, snapping the chain of my thought, I have reached through glass and seized him and stamped him on this page. Now he is gone. And yet, there, a few lines above, he still is, "astraddle," his rump "dingy," his head "alertly frozen." A curious trick, possibly useless, but mine.

The grape leaves where they are not in each other's shadows are golden. Flat leaves, they take the sun flatly, and turn the absolute light, sum of the spectrum and source of all life, into the crayon yellow with which children render it. Here and there, wilt transmutes this lent radiance into a glowing orange, and the green of the still tender leaves—for green persists long into autumn, if we look—strains from the sunlight a fine-veined chartreuse. The shadows these leaves cast upon each other, though vagrant and nervous in the wind that sends friendly scavenging rattles scurrying across the roof, are yet quite various and definite, containing innumerable barbaric suggestions of scimitars, flanged spears, prongs, and menacing helmets. The net effect, however, is innocent of menace. On the contrary, its intricate simultaneous suggestion of shelter and openness, warmth and breeze, invites me outward; my eyes venture into the leaves beyond. I am surrounded by leaves. The oak's are tenacious claws of purplish rust; the elm's, scant feathers of a feminine yellow; the sumac's, a savage, toothed blush. I am upheld in a serene and burning universe of leaves. Yet something plucks me back, returns me to that inner darkness where guilt is the sun.

The events need to be sorted out. I am told I behaved wantonly, and it will take time to integrate this unanimous impression with the unqualified righteousness with which our own acts, however admittedly miscalculated, invest themselves. And once the events are sorted out—the actions given motivations, the actors assigned psychologies, the miscalculations tabulated, the abnormalities named, the whole furious and careless growth pruned by explanation and rooted in history and returned, as it were, to Nature—what then? Is not such a return spurious? Can our spirits really enter Time's haven of mortality and sink composedly among the mulching leaves? No: we stand at the intersection of two kingdoms, and there is no advance and no retreat, only a sharpening of the edge where we stand.

I remember most sharply the black of my wife's dress as she left our house to get her divorce. The dress was a soft black sheath, with a V neckline, and Helen always looked handsome in it; it flattered her pallor. This morning she looked especially handsome, her face utterly white with fatigue. Yet her body, that natural thing, ignored our catastrophe, and her shape and gestures were incongruously usual. She kissed me lightly in leaving, and we both felt the humor of this trip's being insufficiently unlike any other of her trips to Boston—to Symphony, to Bonwit's. The same search for the car keys, the same harassed instructions to the complacent baby-sitter, the same little dip and thrust of her head as she settled behind the wheel of her car. And I, satisfied at last, divorced, studied my children with the eyes of one who had left them, examined my house as one does a set of snapshots from an irrevocable time, drove through the turning landscape as a man in asbestos cuts through a fire, met my wife-to-be—weeping yet smiling, stunned yet brave—and felt, unstoppably, to my horror, the inner darkness burst my skin and engulf us both and drown our love. The natural world, where our love had existed, ceased to exist. My heart shied back; it shies back still. I retreated. As I drove back, the leaves of the trees along the road stated their shapes to me. There is no more story to tell. By telephone I plucked my wife back; I clasped the black of her dress to me, and braced for the pain.

It does not stop coming. The pain does not stop coming. Almost every day, a new installment arrives by mail or face or phone. Every time the telephone rings, I expect it to uncoil some new convolution of conse-quence. I have come to hide in this cottage, but even here, there is a telephone, and the scraping sounds of wind and branch and unseen animal are charged with its electric silence. At any moment, it may explode, and the curious beauty of the leaves will be eclipsed again.

In nervousness, I rise, and walk across the floor. A spider like a white asterisk hangs in air in front of my face. I look at the ceiling and cannot see where its thread is attached. The ceiling is smooth plasterboard. The spider hesitates. It feels a huge alien presence. Its exquisite white legs spread warily and of its own dead weight it twirls on its invisible thread. I catch myself in the quaint and antique pose of the fabulist seeking to draw a lesson from a spider, and become self-conscious. I dismiss self-consciousness and do earnestly attend to this minute articulated star hung so pointedly before my face; and am unable to read the lesson. The spider and I inhabit contiguous but incompatible cosmoses. Across the gulf we feel only fear. The telephone remains silent. The spider reconsiders its spinning. The wind continues to stir the sunlight. In walking in and out of this cottage, I have tracked the floor with a few dead leaves, pressed flat like scraps of dark paper.

And what are these pages but leaves? Why do I produce them but to thrust, by some subjective photosynthesis, my guilt into Nature, where there is no guilt? Now the marsh, level as a carpet, is streaked with faint green amid the shades of brown—russet, ochre, tan, *marron*—and on the far side, where the land lifts above tide level, evergreens stab upwards sullenly. Beyond them, there is a low blue hill; in this coastal region, the hills are almost too modest to bear names. But I *see* it; for the first time in months I see it. I see it as a child, fingers gripping and neck straining, glimpses the roof of a house over a cruelly high wall. Under my window, the lawn is lank and green and mixed with leaves shed from a small elm, and I remember how, the first night I came to this cottage, thinking I was leaving my life behind me, I went to bed alone and read, in the way one reads stray books in a borrowed house, a few pages of an old edition of *Leaves of Grass*. And my sleep was a loop, so that in awaking I seemed still in the book, and the light-struck sky quivering through the stripped branches of the young elm seemed another page of Whitman, and I was entirely open, and lost, like a woman in passion, and free, and in love, without a shadow in any corner of my being. It was a beautiful awakening, but by the next night I had returned to my house.

The precise barbaric shadows on the grape leaves have shifted. The angle of illumination has altered. I imagine warmth leaning against the door, and open the door to let it in; sunlight falls flat at my feet like a penitent.

ALICE WALKER

Revolutionary Petunias

Sammy Lou of Rue
sent to his reward
the exact creature who
murdered her husband,
using a cultivator's hoe
with verve and skill;
and laughed fit to kill
in disbelief
at the angry, militant
pictures of herself
the Sonneteers quickly drew:
not any of them people that
she knew.
A backwoods woman
her house was papered with
funeral home calendars and
faces appropriate for a Mississippi
Sunday School. She raised a George,
a Martha, a Jackie and a Kennedy. Also
a John Wesley Junior.
"Always respect the word of God,"
she said on her way to she didn't
know where, except it would be by
electric chair, and she continued
"Don't yall forgit to *water*
my purple petunias."

{ LILY 'SCHEHERAZADE' }

H. E. BATES

The Lily

My Great-uncle Silas used to live in a small stone reed-thatched cottage on the edge of a pine-wood, where nightingales sang passionately in great numbers through early summer nights and on into the mornings and often still in the afternoons. On summer days after rain the air was sweetly saturated with the fragrance of the pines, which mingled subtly with the exquisite honeysuckle scent, the strange vanilla heaviness from the creamy elder-flowers in the garden hedge and the perfume of old pink and white crimped-double roses of forgotten names. It was very quiet there except for the soft, water-whispering sound of leaves and boughs, and the squabbling and singing of birds in the house-thatch and the trees. The house itself was soaked with years of scents, half sweet, half-dimly-sour with the smell of wood smoke, the curious odour of mauve and milk-coloured and red geraniums, of old wine and tea and the earth smell of my Uncle Silas himself.

It was the sort of house to which old men retire to enjoy their last days. Shuffling about in green carpet-slippers, they do nothing but poke the fire, gloomily clip their beards, read the newspapers with their spectacles on upside down, take too much physic, and die of boredom at last.

But my Uncle Silas was different. At the age of ninety-three he was as lively and restless as a young colt. He shaved every morning at half-past five with cold water and a razor older than himself which resembled an antique barbaric bill-hook. He still kept alive within him some gay, devilish spark of audacity which made him attractive to the ladies. He ate too much and he drank too much.

"God strike me if I tell a lie," he used to say, "but I've drunk enough beer, me boyo, to float the fleet and a drop over."

I remember seeing him on a scorching, windless day in July. He ought to have been asleep in the shade with his red handkerchief over his old walnut-coloured face, but when I arrived he was at work on his potato-patch, digging steadily and strongly in the full blaze of the sun.

Hearing the click of the gate he looked up, and seeing me, waved his spade. The potato-patch was at the far end of the long garden, where the earth was warmest under the woodside, and I walked down the long path to it between rows of fat-podded peas and beans and full-fruited bushes of currant and gooseberry. By the house, under the sun-white wall, the sweet-williams and white pinks flamed softly against the hot marigolds and the orange poppies flat opened to drink in the sun.

"Hot," I said.

"Warmish." He did not pause in his strong, rhythmical digging. The potato-patch had been cleared of its crop and the sun-withered haulms had been heaped against the hedge.

"Peas?" I said. The conversation was inevitably laconic.

"Taters," he said. He did not speak again until he had dug to the edge of the wood. There he straightened his back, blew his nose on his red handkerchief, let out a nonchalant flash of spittle, and cocked his eye at me.

"Two crops," he said. "Two crops from one bit o' land. How's that, me boyo? Every heard talk o' that?"

"Never."

"And you'd be telling a lie if you said you had. Because I know you ain't."

He winked at me, with that swift cock of the head and the perky flicker of the lid that had in it all the saucy jauntiness of a youth of twenty. He was very proud of himself. He was doing something extraordinary and he knew it. There was no humbug about him.

Sitting in the low shade of the garden hedge I watched him, waiting for him to finish digging. He was a short, thick-built man, and his old corduroy trousers concertina-folded over his squat legs and his old wine-red waistcoat ruckled up over his heavy chest made him look dwarfer and thicker still. He was as ugly as some old Indian idol, his skin walnut-stained and scarred like a weather-cracked apple, his cheeks hanging loose and withered, his lips wet and almost sensual and a trifle sardonic with their sideways twist and the thick pout of the lower lip. His left eye was bloodshot, a thin vein or two of scarlet staining the white, but he kept the lid half-shut, only raising it abruptly now and then with an odd cocking-flicker that made him look devilish and sinister. The sudden gay, jaunty flash of his eyes was electric, immortal. I told him once that he'd live to be a thousand. "I shall," he said.

When he had finished the digging and was scraping the light sun-dry soil from his spade with his flattened thumb I got up languidly from under the hedge.

"Don't strain yourself," he said.

He shouldered his spade airily and walked away towards the house and I followed him, marvelling at his age, his strength, and his tirelessness under that hot sun. Half-way up the garden path he stopped to show me his gooseberries. They were as large as young green peaches. He gathered a handful, and the bough, relieved of the weight, swayed up swiftly from the earth. When I had taken a gooseberry he threw the rest into his mouth, crunching them like a horse eating fresh carrots. Something made me say, as I sucked the gooseberry:

"You must have been born about the same year as Hardy."

"Hardy?" He cocked his bloodshot eye at me. "What Hardy?"

"Thomas Hardy."

He thought a moment, crunching gooseberries.

"I recollect him. Snotty little bit of a chap, red hair, always had a dew-drop on the end of his nose. One o' them Knotting Fox Hardies. Skinny lot. I recollect him."

"No, not him. I mean another Hardy. Different man."

"Then he was afore my time."

"No, he was about your time. You must have heard of him. He wrote books."

The word finished him: he turned and began to stride off towards the house. "Books," I heard him mutter, "books!" And suddenly he turned on me and curled his wet red lips and said in a voice of devastating scorn, his bloodshot eye half-angry, half-gleeful:

"I daresay." And then in a flash: "But could he grow goosegogs like that?"

Without pausing for an answer, he strode off again, and I followed him up the path and out of the blazing white afternoon sun into the cool, geranium-smelling house, and there he sat down in his shirt-sleeves in the big black-leathered chair that he once told me his grandmother had left him, with a hundred pounds sewn in the seat that he sat on for ten years without knowing it.

"Mouthful o' wine?" he said to me softly, and then before I had time to answer he bawled into the silence of the house:

"Woman! If you're down the cellar bring us a bottle o' cowslip!"

"I'm upstairs," came a voice.

"Then come down. And look slippy."

"Fetch it yourself!"

"What's that, y'old tit? I'll fetch you something you won't forget in a month o' Sundays. D'ye hear?" There was a low muttering and rumbling over the ceiling. "Fetch it yourself," he muttered. "Did ye hear that? Fetch it yourself!"

"I'll fetch it," I said.

"You sit down," he said. "What do I pay a house-keeper for? Sit down. She'll bring it."

I sat down in the broken-backed chair that in summer time always stood by the door, propping it open. The deep roof dropped a strong black shadow across the threshold but outside the sun blazed unbrokenly, with a still, intense mid-summer light. There was no sound or movement from anything except the bees, droll and drunken, as they crawled and tippled down the yellow and blue and dazzling white throats of the flowers. And sitting there waiting for the wine to come up, listening to the bees working down into the heart of the silence, I saw a flash of scarlet in the garden, and said:

"I see the lily's in bloom."

And as though I had startled him, Uncle Silas looked up quickly, almost with suspicion.

"Ah, she's in bloom," he said.

I was wondering why he always spoke of the lily as though it were a woman, when the housekeeper, her unlaced shoes clip-clopping defiantly on the wooden cellar-steps and the brick passage, came in with a green wine-bottle, and, slapping it down on the table, went out again with her head stiffly uplifted, without a word.

"Glasses!" yelled my Uncle Silas.

"Bringing 'em if you can wait!" she shouted back.

"Well, hurry then! And don't fall over yourself!"

She came back a moment or two later with the glasses, which she clapped down on the table just as she had done the wine-bottle, defiantly, without a word. She was a scraggy, frosty-eyed woman, with a tight, almost lipless mouth, and as she stalked out of the door my Uncle Silas leaned across to me and said in a whisper just loud enough for her to hear:

"Tart as a stick of old rhubarb."

"What's that you're saying?" she said at once.

"Never spoke. Never opened me mouth."

"I heard you!"

"Go and put yourself in curling pins, you old straight hook!"

"I'm leaving," she shouted.

"Leave!" he shouted. "And good riddance."

"Who're you talking to, eh? Who're you talking to, you corrupted old devil? You ought to be ashamed of yourself! If you weren't so old I'd warm your breeches till you couldn't sit down. I'm off."

She flashed out, clip-clopping with her untied shoes along the passage and upstairs while he chanted after her, in his devilish, goading voice:

"Tart as a bit of old rhubarb! Tart as a bit of old rhubarb!"

When the house was silent again he looked at me and winked his bloodshot eye and said "Pour out," and I filled the tumblers with the clear sun-coloured wine.

As we drank I said, "You've done it now," and he winked back at me again, knowing that I knew that she had been leaving every day for twenty years, and that they had quarreled with each other day and night for nearly all that time, secretly loving it.

Sitting by the door, sipping the sweet, cold wine, I looked at the lily again. Its strange, scarlet, turk's-cap blossoms had just begun to uncurl in the July heat, the colour hot and passionate against the snow-coloured pinks and the cool larkspurs and the stiff spikes of the madonnas, sweet and virgin, but like white wax. Rare, exotic, strangely lovely, the red lily had blossomed there, untouched, for as long as I could remember.

"When are you going to give me a little bulb off the lily?" I said.

"You know what I've always told you," he said. "You can have her when I'm dead. You can come and dig her up then. Do what you like with her."

I nodded. He drank, and as I watched his skinny throat filling and relaxing with the wine I said:

"Where did you get it? In the first place?"

He looked at the almost empty glass.

"I pinched her," he said.

"How?"

"Never mind. Give us another mouthful o' wine."

He held out his glass, and I rose and took the wine-bottle from the table and paused with my hand on the cork. "Go on," I said, "tell me."

"I forget," he said. "It's been so damn long ago."

"How long?"

"I forget," he said.

As I gave him back his wine-filled glass I looked at him with a smile and he smiled back at me, half-cunning, half-sheepish, as though he knew what I was thinking. He possessed the vividest memory, a memory he often boasted about as he told me the stories of his boyhood, rare tales of prize-fights on summer mornings by isolated woods very long ago, of how he heard the news of the Crimea, of how he took a candle to church to warm his hands against it in the dead of winter, and how when the parson cried out "And he shall see a great light, even as I see one now!" he snatched up the candle in fear of hell and devils and sat on it. "And I can put my finger on the spot now."

By that smile on his face I knew that he remembered about the lily, and after taking another long drink of the wine he began to talk. His voice was crabbed and rusty, a strong, ugly voice that had no softness or tenderness in it, and his half-shut, bloodshot eye and his wet, curled lips looked rakish and wicked, as though he were acting the villainous miser in one of those travelling melodramas of his youth.

"I seed her over in a garden, behind a wall," he said. "Big wall, about fifteen feet high. We were banging in hard a-carrying hay and I was on the top o' the cart and could see her just over the wall. Not just one—scores, common as poppies. I felt I shouldn't have no peace again until I had one. And I nipped over the wall that night about twelve o'clock and ran straight into her."

"Into the lily?"

"Tah! Into a gal. See? Young gal—about my age, daughter o' the house. All dressed in thin white. 'What are you doing here?' she says, and I believe she was as frit as I was. 'I lost something,' I says. 'It's all right. You know me.' And then she wanted to know what I'd lost, and I felt as if I didn't care what happened, and I said, 'Lost my head, I reckon.' And she laughed, and then I laughed and then she said, 'Ssshhh! Don't you see I'm as done as you are if we're found here? You'd better go. What did you come for, anyway?' And I told her. She wouldn't believe me. 'It's right,' I says, 'I just come for the lily.' And she just stared at me. 'And you know what they do to people who steal?' she says. 'Yes,' I says, and they were the days when you could be hung for looking at a sheep almost. 'But picking flowers ain't stealing,' I says. 'Sshhh!' she says again. 'What d'ye think I'm going to say if they find me here? Don't talk so loud. Come here behind these trees and keep quiet.' And we went and sat down behind some old box-trees and she kept whispering about the lily and telling me to whisper for fear anyone should come. 'I'll get you the lily all right,' she says, 'if you keep quiet. I'll dig it up.'"

He ceased talking, and after the sound of his harsh, uncouth racy voice the summer afternoon seemed quieter than ever, the drowsy, stumbling boom of the bees in the July flowers only deepening the hot drowsy silence. I took a drink of the strong, cool, flower-odoured wine and waited for my Uncle Silas to go on with the story, but nothing happened, and finally I looked up at him.

"Well?" I said. "What happened?"

For a moment or two he did not speak. But finally he turned and looked at me with a half-solemn, half-vivacious expression, one eye half-closed, and told me in a voice at once dreamy, devilish, innocent, mysterious, and triumphant, all and more than I had asked to know.

"She gave me the lily," he said.

MARK DOTY

In the Community Garden

It's almost over now,
late summer's accomplishment,
and I can stand face to face

with this music,
eye to seed-paved eye
with the sunflowers' architecture:

such muscular leaves,
the thick stems' surge.
Though some are still

shiningly confident,
others can barely
hold their heads up;

their great leaves wrap the stalks
like lowered shields. This one
shrugs its shoulders;

this one's in a rush
to be nothing but form.
Even at their zenith,

you could see beneath the gold
the end they'd come to.
So what's the use of elegy?

If their work
is this skyrocket passage
through the world,

is it mine to lament them?
Do you think they'd want
to bloom forever?

It's the trajectory they desire—
believe me, they do
desire, you could say they are

one intent, finally,
to be this leaping
green, this bronze haze

bending down. How could they stand
apart from themselves
and regret their passing,

when they are a field
of lifting and bowing faces,
faces ringed in flames?

{ HOSTA 'JUNE' }

JOSEPHINE JACOBSEN

Jack Frost

Mrs. Travis was drinking a sturdy cup of tea. She sat in the wicker rocker on her back porch, in a circle of sun, after picking Mrs. James her flowers. Exhausted, she felt a little tired, and she rested with satisfaction. Mrs. James's motley bouquet sat by her knee, in one of the flower tins.

Mrs. Travis wore a blue cotton dress with a man's suitcoat over it, and around that a tie, knotted for a belt. Her legs were bare, but her small feet had on them a pair of child's galoshes, the sort that have spring buckles. Since several springs were missing, she wore the galoshes open, and sometimes they impeded her.

Half of her back porch, the left-hand side, was clear, and held her wicker rocker with its patches of sprung stiff strands; but the other half was more fruitful, a great pile of possessions which she needed, or had needed, or in certain possible circumstances might come to need: a tin footbath containing rope, twine, and a nest of tin containers from the insides of flower baskets; a hatchet; a galosh for the right foot; garden tools; a rubber mat; a beekeeper's helmet for the black-fly season. Nearby, a short length of hose; chunks of wood. The eye flagged before the count.

There was a small winding path, like the witch's in a fairy tale, between cosmos so tall they brushed the shoulders. To its right almost immediately, vegetables grew: the feathery tops of carrots, dusty beet-greens, a few handsome mottled zucchini, the long runners of beans. Last year there had still been tomatoes, but the staking-up and coaxing had become too much; she said to herself instead that such finicking had come to bore her. To the left of the cosmos, below a small slope of scratchy lawn, was the garden proper—on this mellow September afternoon a fine chaos of unchosen color, the Mexican shades of zinnias, the paper-cutout heads of dahlias, a few grown-over roses, more cosmos, the final spikes of some fine gladioli, phlox running heavily back to magenta, and closer to the cooling ground, the pink and purple of asters. There were even a few pansies, wildly persisting in a tangle of grass and weeds.

Until a few years ago her younger brother Henry had driven over two hundred miles, up from Connecticut, to help her plant both gardens, but Henry had died at eighty-two. Mrs. Travis herself did not actually know how old she was. She believed herself to be ninety-three; but having several years ago gone suddenly to check the fact of the matter in the faint gray handwriting of her foxed Bible, a cup of strong tea in her hand, she had sloshed the tea as she peered, and then on the puffed, run surface, she could no longer read the final digit. 3? 7? 1883? Just possibly, 1887? For a moment she felt youth pressing on her; if it were, if it possibly were 1887, several years had lifted themselves off. There they were, still to come with all the variety of their days. Turn those to hours, those to minutes, and it was a gigantic fresh extension. But she thought the fig-ure was a 3. It was the last time she looked in the back of the Bible.

Tacked onto the porch wall was a large calendar; each day past was circled in red. Only three such showed; she would circle September 4th when she closed the door for the night.

Now before she could swallow the last of her tea, here came Mrs. James's yellow sweater, borne on a bicycle along the dirt road outside the hedge. Dismounted, Mrs. James wheeled the bicycle up the path and leaned it against the porch post. She was sweaty with effort over the baked ridges of the road, and, half a century younger than her hostess, she radi-ated summer-visitor energy and cheer.

"Oh Mrs. Travis!" she cried. "You've got them all ready! Aren't they lovely!" She was disappointed, since she had hoped to choose the picking; but she and her summer friends regarded Mrs. Travis's activity as much like that of Dr. Johnson's dog walking on its hind legs.

Mrs. Travis looked with satisfaction at the jumble of phlox, gladioli, dahlias, and zinnias which, with all the slow, slow bending and straightening, had cost her an hour.

"Oh, its so *warm*," said Mrs. James with pleasure, sitting down on the step at Mrs. Travis's feet.

Mrs. Travis had so few occasions to speak that it always seemed to take her a minute to call up her voice, which arrived faint with distance. "Yes," she said, almost inaudibly. "It's a very good day."

"Oh look!" said Mrs. James, pleased. "Look how well the rose begonia's doing!" She had given it to Mrs. Travis early in the summer, it was one of her own bulbs from California, and she could see its full gorgeousness now, blooming erratically beside the path, hanging its huge rosy bloom by the gap-toothed rake and a tiny pile of debris: twigs, dead grass, a few leaves.

Mrs. Travis did not answer, but Mrs. James saw it was because she was looking at the begonia's gross beauty with a powerful smugness. They sat companionably for a moment. Mrs. James seemed to Mrs. Travis like one of the finches, or yellow-headed warblers, which frequented her for the warmest weeks. Exactly as she thought so, Mrs. James said, suddenly sad, "Do you know the birds are all going, *already*?"

"No, not all," said Mrs. Travis soothingly. "The chickadees won't go." But Mrs. Travis did not really care; it was the flowers she created out of nothing.

"I hate to see them go so soon," said Mrs. James, stubbornly sad.

"But you'll be going, too," said Mrs. Travis, faintly and comfortingly.

Mrs. James, lifting her chin, looked at Mrs. Travis. "Are you going to stay here all winter, *again*?" she asked.

Mrs. Travis looked at her with stupefaction. Then she said, "Yes." She was afraid Mrs. James was going to repeat what she had said for the past two autumns, about Mrs. Travis moving into the village for the winter; here she was, no phone, no close neighbors; nothing but snow, and ice, and wind, and the grocery boy with his little bag, and the mailman's Pontiac passing without stopping. But Mrs. James said only, "Look, here comes Father O'Rourke."

There was the clap of a car door, and Father O'Rourke appeared between the cosmos, surprisingly wearing his dog collar, his black coat slung over his white shoulder. Mrs. James stood up, pleased that Mrs. Travis had a visitor. "I've got to get these flowers back," she said. Now came the embarrassing moment. "How—er, they're so lovely; what . . . ?"

"That's three dollars for the pailful," said Mrs. Travis with satisfaction. Mrs. James, whose grandmother, as a little girl, had known Mrs. Travis in Boston, continued to feel, no matter what she paid, that the flowers had come as a gift from Mrs. Travis's conservatory. She laid three dollars inconspicuously on the table by the oil lamp, and Mrs. Travis watched her and Father O'Rourke saying hello, and goodbye for the winter, to each other in the hot slanting sun.

As Mrs. James wheeled her bicycle away, Father O'Rourke replaced her on the step. He did not offer to shake hands, having noticed that such gestures seemed to distract Mrs. Travis, as some sort of clumsy recollected maneuver. He had just come from making the final plans for the Watkins wedding, and fresh from all that youth and detail, he looked at Mrs. Travis, whose pale small blue eyes looked back at him, kindly, but from a long distance. The purpose of Father O'Rourke's visit embarrassed him; he was afraid of Mrs. Travis's iron will.

"What a lot of flowers you've still got," began Father O'Rourke, obliquely.

Mrs. Travis looked out over the ragged rainbow on the slope. The sun, at its western angle, was still a good bit above the smaller of the big dark mountains behind which it would go. "Oh yes," she said, "they'll be here for a long time. A couple of weeks, probably." He saw that she meant just that.

"Well," he said, "you know, Mrs. Travis, after five years here, I've found we just don't know. Things may go on almost to October; and then, again, a night in late August will do it."

Mrs. Travis did not reply to this, and Father O'Rourke plunged. "I saw Mrs. Metcalfe at the post office this morning," he said, looking placatingly at Mrs. Travis's profile. "Did you know that she's finished making that big sitting room off her south porch into that little apartment she's going to rent out?"

Mrs. Travis, who had had enough of this for one day, indeed for one lifetime, turned her head and looked him straight in his hazel eye.

"I'm not going anywhere," she said, surprisingly loud, adding from some past constraint, "Father O'Rourke."

A final sense of the futility of his effort struck him silent. They sat quietly for a few seconds. What on earth am I trying to do? he thought suddenly. Why *should* she move? Well, so many reasons; he wondered if they were all worthless. He knew that, before he was born, Mrs. Travis had enlisted in the army of five eccentric hermits, isolates, writing their own terms into some curious treaty. But she was so much older than anyone else that the details became more and more obscure; also, more romanticized. There was even doubt as to a dim and distant husband. A fallen or faithless lover appeared, along with factual but tinted tales of early privilege. But the Miss Havisham motif he tended to discount; it was so widely beloved.

All he knew for certain was that, with Mrs. Travis, he was in the presence of an authenticity of elimination which caused him a curiously mingled horror and envy. At times he thought that her attention, fiercely concentrated, brought out, like a brilliant detail from an immense canvas, a quality of some nonverbal and passionate comprehension. At other times he saw a tremendously old woman, all nuances of the world, her past, and the earth's present, ignored or forgotten; brittle and single, everything rejected but her own tiny circle of motion.

With a fairly complex mind, Father O'Rourke combined a rather simple set of hopes, not many of which were realized. One of these was to enter Mrs. Travis's detail, as some sort of connection with a comfort, or even a lack of finality. The bond between them, actually, was a belief in the physical, a conviction of the open-ended mystery of matter. But since Mrs. Travis had never been a Catholic, that particular avenue wasn't open to him. Her passion was in this scraggy garden, but he distinguished that it was coldly unsentimental, unlike that of most lady gardeners he knew. He was not sure just how Mrs. Travis did feel about her flowers. He considered that, in homily and metaphor, the garden-thing—Eden to Gethsemane—had been overdone; nevertheless, in connection with Mrs. Travis, he always thought of it. He had, on a previous visit last month, brought up some flower passages from the Bible; but the only interest she had shown was by a question as to which type of lily the lilies-of-the-field had been. She had at least five kinds, lifting their slick and sappy stalks above confusion. But when he had said they were most like anemones, she had lost interest, having forgotten, after fifty years in the New Hampshire mountains, what anemones looked like.

"I have to go back to the Watkinses again tomorrow," said Father O'Rourke. He knew he should have been back at the rectory half an hour ago. Here he sat, mesmerized somehow by the invisible movement of the sun across the step, by the almost total stillness. It was cooling rapidly, too. He picked up his coat and hunched his arms into it. "Can I bring you anything, then?"

"No," she said. She was sorry to see him go. She

turned her head to look fully at him. "Do you want any flowers?" she asked.

He hesitated, thinking of Mrs. Metcalfe's pious arrangement, three pink gladioli in a thin-stemmed glass on each side of the altar. "Well," he said, "how about some zinnias for my desk? I'll pick them tomorrow," he added hastily, as he saw her eyes cloud, rallying for action. On the step he lingered, smiling at her. Oppressed. "Well," he said idiotically, "don't let Jack Frost get your flowers."

She watched him attentively down the path. Just as his starter churned, the sun left the porch and, looking up to the mountain, Mrs. Travis saw that it had gone for the day.

She went in at once, forgetting her rake, lying in the garden, her empty teacup, and the three dollars on the table, but carrying a short chunk of wood under each arm. She took at least one each time she went into the house. She never turned on the furnace before October, but there was a small chunk stove in the corner, by the lamp table, and it warmed the room in a matter of minutes. She decided to have supper right now. She had a chop, and there was still some lettuce. She had picked a fine head this morning; it was right in the colander, earth still clinging to its bottom.

By eight o' clock it had got very cold outside. But the room was warm. Mrs. Travis went to sleep in her chair. Sleep often took her now with ferocious touch, so that everything just disappeared; and when she woke up, she found that hours had passed. On a warm night in July she had slept in her chair all night long, waking up, disoriented, to a watery dawn.

Now she not only slept, she dreamed. An unpleasant dream, something extremely unusual. She was in a dark huge city lit by thin lamps, and she was afraid. She was afraid of a person, who might be coming toward her, or coming up behind her. And yet, more than a person— though she knew it was a man in a cap. She must get into a house before he found her. Or before he found someone else. A strange-looking girl went by her, hurrying, very pale, with a big artificial rose in her hair. She turned suddenly into an opening on the dreamer's right; it was the darkest of alleys and the dreamer hurried faster than ever. Ahead of her, in the fog, she could see the dimly lit sign of an inn; but as she hurried faster, a terrible scream, high and short, came out of the alley. It woke Mrs. Travis, her hands locked hard on the arms of the chair.

She sat quite still, looking around the familiar room. Then memory handed her one of the clear messages that now so seldom arrived. The Lodger. That was just it. She had suddenly, after all these years, had a dream about Jack the Ripper, as she had had several times when she first read of his foggy city streets a very long time ago. But why this dream should have escaped from the past to molest her, she could not think.

The little fire in the stove was out, but the stove itself still ticked and settled with heat. The wall clock said two minutes to eight. Stiff from sleep, Mrs. Travis reached over and turned the dial of the small discolored radio under the table lamp, and immediately a loud masculine voice said, " . . . front, all the way from the Great Lakes, throughout northern New England, and into Canada. Frost warnings have been issued for the mountain areas of Vermont and New Hampshire. Tomorrow the unseasonable cold will continue, for a chilly Labor Day; but by Wednesday . . . " Appalled, Mrs. Travis switched off the evil messenger.

Frost. It was not that it was so strange; it was so sudden. She could still feel the heat of the sun, on the porch, on her hands and her ankles. Two weeks, she had thought.

As she sat, staring for a moment straight ahead, a brand new fury started up, deep inside her. Two weeks. It was an eternity of summer. The long nights, the brutal chill, the endless hardness of the earth, they were reasonable enough, in their time. In their time. But this was her time, and they were about to invade it. She began to tremble with anger. She thought of her seeds, and how dry and hard they had been; of her deathlike bulbs, slipping old skin, with everything locked inside them, and she, her body, had turned them into that summer of color and softness and good smells that was out there in the dark garden.

She turned her head, right and left, looking for an exit for her rage. Then suddenly she sat forward in her chair. An idea had come to her with great force and clarity. It grew in the room, like an enormous plant covered with buds. Mrs. Travis knew exactly what she was going to do. Her intention was not protective, but defiant; her sense was of battle, punitive battle.

She stood up carefully, and went and got the flashlight from the shelf over the woodbox. She went to the porch door and opened it, and then closed it hastily behind her, protecting the room's warmth. There was no sound or light in any direction, but there was a diffused brightness behind the mountain's darker bulk. She tipped over the pail that had held Mrs. James's flowers, so that the leafy water poured down the sloping porch. Then she began fitting the tin flower-holders into it. She could not get them all in, and she took her pail into the house and came back for the last three. She arranged the pail and the tins on the kitchen floor, and then she attached a short length of hose to the cold water spigot, dropped the other end in the pail, and turned on the water. She filled the big tins the same way, and then lifted the small ones into the sink, removing the hose, and filled them. Turning with satisfaction to look through the doorway at the clock, she was disconcerted to see that it said five minutes after nine. She stared at it, skeptical but uncertain. It could *stop*; but surely it couldn't skip *ahead*. Perhaps she had mistaken the earlier time. She began to move more rapidly; though she was so excited, all her faculties had come so strongly into one intention, that it seemed to her that she was already moving at a furious pace.

She went over to the kitchen door and took off its hook a felt hat and an ancient overcoat of Henry's. She put the hat on her head, got carefully into the overcoat and stuffed her flashlight into the pocket. She took down from the top of the refrigerator a cracked paper-mâché tray Mrs. James had sent her several Christmases ago; its design of old coins had almost disappeared. At an open drawer she hesitated over a pair of shears. Lately she had found them hard to open and close, and after standing there for half a minute, she took a thick-handled knife instead. She went to look at the empty sitting room and then moved back through the kitchen faster than seemed possible.

Out on the porch, a square of light came through the window, and looking up, she could make out a cloud over the mountain, its edges stained with brightness.

She lit her flashlight, and went cautiously down the step and along the path, carrying her tray under her arm. Faces of cosmos, purple and pink, loomed at her as she went; but even in her tremendous excitement, she knew she couldn't bring in everything, and she went on, the tops of her galoshes making a little flapping noise in the silence. She turned carefully down the slight slope, and here were the zinnias, towered over by the branchy dahlias. She laid her tray on the ground.

But now, breathing more rapidly, she saw that she was in trouble. To cut with her knife, she had to hold the flower's stem, and she had to hold her flashlight to see it, and she had two hands. Fiercely she looked about for an idea; and at just that moment, a clear thin light streamed over the edge of the cloud and lit her. The moon was full. She might have known; that was when a black frost always came.

Mrs. Travis made an inarticulate sound of fierce

pleasure and dropped the flashlight into the tray. Then she began to cut the flowers, working as fast as she could, giving little pants of satisfaction as the shapes heaped themselves up below her. Inch by inch she moved along the ragged rows, pushing, with a galoshed toe, the tray along the ground before her. She cut all the gladioli, even the ones which were still mostly flaccid green tips; she cut all the dahlias, even the buds, and every zinnia. She felt light and warm, and drunk with resistant power. Finally the tray was so full that blooms began to tip over and fall into the cold grass.

Very cautiously indeed she got the tray up, but she could not hold it level and manipulate the flashlight. It made no difference. The moon, enormous and fully round, had laid light all over the garden; the house's shadow was black, as though a pale sun were shining.

Teetering a little to hold the tray level, Mrs. Travis went up the path, carefully up the step. She set the tray on the table, knocking over her dirty teacup and saucer, and each broke cleanly in two pieces. She stepped over them, opened the door on warmth, and went back for her load.

First she filled the pail; then every tin. There was a handful of zinnias left, and a pile of phlox. Threatened, Mrs. Travis looked about the kitchen, but saw nothing helpful. She could feel her cheeks burning in the room's summer, and with a little noise of triumph, she went through the door to the bedroom and came back with the big china chamber pot. It had a fine network of fractured veins, and on it was a burst of painted magenta foliage. When she had filled it under the tap it was too heavy to lift down, so she stuffed in the flowers and left it there. A small chartreuse-colored spider began to run up and down the sink's edge.

Then, just as she was turning to look at all she had done, like a cry from an alley, like a blow between the shoulders, to her mind's eye came the rose begonia. She could positively see in the air before her its ruffled heavy head, the coral flush of its crowded petals; from its side sprang the bud, color splitting the sheath. The bulb had thrust it up, and there it was, out there.

Though she felt as though she were drunk, she also felt shrewd. Think of the low ones you can't stoop to tonight, she thought, the nasturtiums, the pansies, the bachelor's buttons, the ragged robins. But it made no difference. She knew that unless she took the rose begonia, she had lost everything. She looked at the clock; it was half past ten. She could be back in ten minutes; and she decided that then she would sit right down by the stove and sleep there, deliberately, and not move into the cold bed and take off bit by bit so many clothes.

There were four sticks of wood by the stove, and under the lid the embers were bright. She put in three sticks; then she went empty handed to the porch. It was very cold and absolutely still. The moon was even brighter; it was almost halfway up the sky. She found a terra-cotta flowerpot on the porch corner, and she rooted in the footbath until she found her trowel. Then she went, as fast as she could go, down the path to the halfway point, where she came upon the rose begonia, paled by the chill of the light. As she bent over, her head roared; so she kneeled, and drove the blunt trowel-edge into the earth.

When the roots came up in a great ball of earth she pressed them into the pot, stuffing more clods of fibrous earth around them. Then she started to get up. But with the pot in one hand and the trowel in the other, it was impossible.

She dropped the trowel. She did not even think that she could get it tomorrow. Suddenly she was cold to her very teeth. She thought just of the room, the hot, col-ored, waiting room. Holding the pot in her left hand, pushing with her right, she got herself upright; but it made her dizzy, and as she lurched a little to the side the rake's teeth brought her down in a heavy fall. The flower shot from her hand and disappeared into the shadows and a bright strong pain blasted her. It was her ankle; and she lay with her face close to the cold dirt, feeling the waves of pain hit her.

Mrs. Travis raised her head, to see how far away the porch was. It was perhaps ten or eleven yards. Another country. Things seemed dimmer, too, and wrenching her head sideways and up, she saw that the huge moon had shrunk; it sat high and small, right at the top of the sky.

Mrs. Travis lowered her head gently and began to crawl, pushing with her hands and the knee of her good leg. She went along, inch by inch, foot by foot; she had no fear, since there was an absolute shield between one second and the next.

The porch was so shadowed now that she nearly

missed it; the step struck her advancing hand. It took her three tries, but she got up over it, and went on, inch by inch, toward the door. A sliver of china bit her hand. Bright light came through the keyhole. She reached up and easily turned the doorknob; then like a crab she was across the sill.

She could not, she found, turn; but she pushed out with her left foot, and miraculously the door clicked shut just behind her. She felt no pain at all, but there was something forming under her ribs.

In the room's heat, the foliage of the marigolds gave out a spicy smell, stronger than the fragrance of the phlox. A dozen shapes and colors blazed before her eyes, and a great tearing breath came up inside her like an explosion. Mrs. Travis lifted her head, and the whole wave of summer, advancing obedient and glorious, in a crest of color and warmth and fragrance broke right over her.

KATHLEEN RAINE

Winifred's Garden

For Winifred Nicholson

Dear Bank's Head, in high summer overgrown
With garden-flowers run wild
And wild flowers chosen
Each for some beauty, to be a painter's friend
—Yellow Welsh poppy, Heart's Ease, Dusky Cranesbill
Woodruff and columbine—
I well remember when this tangle of flowers at ease,
Now song-birds' ambush, was a more tended place
Than now, when some new prize was set in place
That now blooms unregarded, or with a thought
Of in the autumn clearing to make room.
And yet your wise hand knows to spare,
Knows to let time weave on
Its tapestry of leaf and flower and song
Under your pearly northern sky.
We grow old, you and I, your garden
Dreams on its way from memory to sleep. Someday
And will be gone
But memories strewn like floating seed in many lives
Of such a day as this, and other days
Caught between the planned and the realised
Poised on the butterfly-wings of hovering paradise.

Biographical Notes on the Authors

MARY AUSTIN (1868-1934) was born in Illinois and later made her home in California, where she became a noted conservationist and a founder of the Carmel literary colony. She is the author of numerous works of fiction, including *The Land of Little Rain* (1903), *The Basket Woman* (1904), *A Woman of Genius* (1917), *No. 26 Jayne Street* (1920), and *One Smoke Stories* (1934). Her autobiography, *Earth Horizon*, was published in 1932.

H. E. BATES (1905-1974) was a British journalist, novelist, and short story writer who often explored themes of English country life. His books include *My Uncle Silas* (1940), *The Jacaranda Tree* (1948), *A Moment in Time* (1964), and *The Blossoming World* (1971).

KATE CHOPIN (1850-1904) was born in St. Louis, Missouri, but spent many years living in Louisiana. Her collections of stories depicting Bayou Creoles and Cajuns, *Bayou Folk* (1894) and *A Night in Acadie* (1897), established her as a major writer of Southern regional literature. Today, she is best known for her early feminist novella, *The Awakening* (1899).

AMY CLAMPITT (1920-1994) grew up in New Providence, Iowa, and lived most of her adult life in New York City, where she worked as a freelance editor until her own writing brought her recognition and new opportunities. For many years, she spent her summers in the remote seaside village of Corea, Maine, an important source of inspiration for her poetry. Clampitt was sixty-three when her first collection, *The Kingfisher,* was published. Four volumes quickly followed in the eleven years before her death: *What the Light Was Like* (1985), *Archaic Figure* (1987), *Westward* (1990), and *A Silence Opens* (1994). During her short career, Clampitt was honored often, and in 1992 she was awarded a MacArthur Fellowship. Recently her *Collected Poems* has been published, along with two volumes of her collected essays.

EUGENIA COLLIER (b. 1928) is a native of Baltimore and grew up in the racially segregated inner city. Educated at Howard University, Columbia University, and the University of Maryland, she became a literary critic and a professor of English, concentrating on African American literature. Among her published works are the anthology *Afro-American Writing* (co-editor, Richard A. Long) and a story collection, *Breeder and Other Stories.* "Marigolds," reprinted here, was her first published story. Ms. Collier writes: "In the inner city, flowers were grown in cramped little window boxes. They were expressions of people's need to create beauty. I discovered my fervor for planting, nurturing, and growing beautiful things when I was able to move from an apartment to a house with a spacious yard. Marigolds were my favorites because they so enthusiastically yielded their glory without having to be fussed over and given special treatment. At a difficult time of my life, I remembered the fresh scent of marigolds and their sunny blossoms, and how even in poor soil and adverse conditions they could make barren places beautiful. The story 'Marigolds' combines my love for African American culture, my joy in gardening, and the need to assuage the pain of a bad time in my life. Although I have written many stories since, 'Marigolds' remains one of my favorites."

BILLY COLLINS (b. 1941) is the award-winning author of many books of poetry, including *Picnic, Lightning*; *Questions About Angels*; *The Art of Drowning*; and *Sailing Alone Around the Room: New and Selected Poems.* His poems have been selected many times for the annual *Best American Poetry* anthology.

MARK DOTY (b. 1953) has published many volumes of poems, including *My Alexandria*, winner of the National Book Critics Circle Award and the T. S. Eliot Prize; and *Atlantis*, winner of the Ambassador Book Award, the Bingham Poetry Prize, and a Lambda Literary Award. He is also the author of two books of memoirs, *Heaven's Coast* and *Firebird*.

ROBERT FROST (1874-1963), a major modern American poet, often draws on his knowledge of the life and landscape of rural New England, where he lived. Among his books of poetry are *A Boy's Will* (1913), *New Hampshire* (1923), *Steeple Bush* (1947), and *In the Clearing* (1962). Frost was a four-time winner of the Pulitzer Prize.

ROBERT GRAVES (1895-1985), English poet, novelist, and classical scholar, is the author of many volumes, including the historical novels *I, Claudius* (1934) and *Homer's Daughter* (1955), as well as the important critical works *The White Goddess* (1947) and *Greek Myths and Legends* (1968).

O. HENRY (1862-1910) was born in Greensboro, North Carolina, and began writing short stories in prison in 1897 during a three-year sentence for embezzling a small amount of money. On his release, he moved to New York City, where he often wrote more than one story a week, producing ten collections in as many years and establishing himself as one of the best-known and best-loved American story writers. *The Complete Works of O. Henry* was published in 1953.

JOSEPHINE JACOBSEN (b. 1908) is a poet, literary critic, and short story writer. She has been the recipient of many awards, including the Lenore Marshall Poetry Prize, a nomination for the National Book Award, and the American Academy of Arts

Citation in 1994. She is the author of *What Goes Without Saying: Collected Stories; The Instinct of Knowing: Lectures, Criticism and Occasional Prose;* and *In the Crevice of Time: New and Collected Poems.*

SARAH ORNE JEWETT (1849-1909) was born in South Berwick, Maine. She is the author of novels and many short stories, nearly all set in her native state. Among them are *Deephaven* (1877), *A Country Doctor* (1884), and *The Country of the Pointed Firs* (1896).

HOWARD NEMEROV (1920-1991), poet, novelist, and literary critic, was born in New York City. *The Collected Poems of Howard Nemerov* (1977) won both the Pulitzer Prize and a National Book Award. He was appointed National Poet Laureate in 1988.

SYLVIA PLATH (1932-1963) as born in Boston and graduated from Smith College. She is the author of *The Colossus* (1960), and *Ariel* (1964), as well as several volumes of journals and letters and the widely read novel *The Bell Jar* (1971).

KATHLEEN RAINE (b. 1908) is a British poet and scholar. She has published twelve volumes of poems, including her *Collected Poems* (2001). An internationally respected critic of William Blake and W. B. Yeats, she is the author of books on both writers and of an autobiography, *The Inner Journey of the Poet.*

CHRISTOPHER REID (b. 1949) was Poetry Editor at Faber and Faber in London from 1991 to 1999. *Mermaids Explained,* a selection from five books of his poems, was published in 2001. His book of poems for children, *All Sorts,* won the Signal Award in 2000.

SAKI (1870-1916) was born in Burma (Myanmar) and educated in England. In 1894 he began writing satirical sketches for the *Westminster Gazette*. These were collected in a volume entitled *The Westminster Alice* (1902). Saki died in action in France at the beginning of the First World War. His fiction, *The Short Stories of Saki,* was published posthumously in 1930.

WILLIAM SAROYAN (1908-1981) was born in Armenia. Among his many published works are the novel *The Human Comedy* (1943), the short story collection *My Name Is Aram* (1940), and the play *The Time of Your Life,* winner of both the Drama Critics Circle Award and the Pulitzer Prize in 1940.

JAMES SCHUYLER (1923-1991) was born in Chicago and settled in New York City, where he was one of the important poets of the New York School. An avid gardener, he frequently used gardening themes in his poetry. Among his many collections are *Hymn to Life* (1974), the Pulitzer Prize-winning *The Morning of the Poem* (1981), *A Few Days* (1985), and *Collected Poems* (1993).

JOHN UPDIKE (b. 1932) was born in Shillington, Pennsylvania. He is a novelist, poet, and distinguished critic. Among his many novels are *The Centaur; Couples; Bech: A Book; The Witches of Eastwick;* and the Rabbit Angstrom trilogy *Rabbit, Run; Rabbit at Rest;* and *Rabbit Returns.*

ARTURO VIVANTE (b. 1923) grew up near Siena, Italy, and immigrated to the United States in the 1950s. Although he has always written in English, he is sustained by his native Italy, which is the setting in most of his stories. More than seventy short stories have been published in *The New Yorker.* His most recent collection is *The Tales of Arturo Vivante.*

ALICE WALKER (b. 1944) is a novelist, essayist, and poet. The daughter of sharecroppers, she grew up in Eatonville, Georgia, where her mother's gardens were famous. Among her published books are the short story collections *In Love & Trouble* and *The Way Forward Is With a Broken Heart*, the Pulitzer-Prize-winning novel *The Color Purple*, and the collection of essays *In Search of Our Mothers' Gardens: The Legacy of Southern Black Women*.

WILLIAM CARLOS WILLIAMS (1883-1963) was a practicing physician in his hometown of Rutherford, New Jersey, as well as the author of many poems, plays, short stories, essays, and an autobiography. His major works include *In the American Grain* (1956); *Pictures from Brueghel and Other Poems* (1962), winner of the Pulitzer Prize; and *Collected Poems* in two volumes (1986, 1988).

CYNTHIA ZARIN (b. 1959) is the author of three books of poems, *The Swordfish Tooth*, *Fire Lyric*, and *The Zoo in Winter*, as well as several books for children. She has been honored by grants from the National Endowment for the Arts, the Ingram-Merrill Foundation, and the Peter I. Lavan Foundation. She is Artist-in-Residence at the Cathedral of St. John the Divine in New York City.

The Editors

CHARLES DEAN was born in Augusta, Georgia, where his grandmother once planted her entire lawn in petunias. Raised in Knoxville, Tennessee, he graduated from the University of Tennessee with a major in philosophy. For many years he has been the assistant maître d' at Manhattan's Carlyle Hotel restaurant. He designs and maintains curbside gardens for his New York City apartment building and grows cryptanthus plants on his windowsills.

CLYDE WACHSBERGER grew up in Riverdale, New York. He graduated from Columbia University intending to be an archaeologist but discovered that he preferred digging in the garden. He is a landscape designer and manages the greenhouses for Ornamental Plantings Nursery in Southold, New York. He has had several one-man shows of his watercolors featuring Long Island gardens and landscapes. His memoir, "Mr. Soito's Peonies," appeared in *Global City Review*, and he writes a monthly garden essay for *North Fork Country*. He is a recipient of a grant for writing from the Ludwig Vogelstein Foundation.